GEORGIA'S DOC HOLLIDAY

By Olin Jackson

Published by Whippoorwill Publications
3617 Summit Oaks Drive
Roswell, Georgia, 30075

First Edition Published 2006

Library of Congress Control Number: 2004012345

International Standard Book Number: 0-9776988-0-7

Card Cataloging In Progress:

For additional copies:
Whippoorwill Publications
3617 Summit Oaks Dr.
Roswell, Georgia 30075
Toll-Free: 877-673-4063

D0916643

John Henry Holliday, 1879, Prescott, Arizona.

Acknowledgements

Grateful appreciation is hereby extended to the numerous individuals who assisted in the development and accumulation of material contained in this book, including Gene Carlisle, Bill Dunn, Jackie Kennedy, Edward Jordan Lanham, Karen Holliday Tanner, Victoria Wilcox, and Karen Spears Zacharias.

To Judy...For putting up with me in our many travels together.

Contents

The Early Days in Georgia

As of this writing, John Henry "Doc" Holliday has been dead for well over a century, but his legend is more profound and widely-known today than ever before. He was born in Griffin, Georgia, and spent a fair amount of time in the Atlanta area, living with relatives and later practicing dentistry. One of the homes at which he spent this time still stands in Fayetteville, Georgia.

Many Southerners have often claimed that historians – particularly historians from the North – were nothing more than myth-makers when it came to documenting "factual" information about the South. When faced with yet another "accurate portrayal" of local history told from an outsider's limited perspective, the Southerner often leans back in a rocker and chides the historian saying, "Well, friend, that's your tale and I'm a'settin' on mine."

In fairness, while these historians have been known to rewrite history, Southerners have been known for embellishing it. When the two forces are combined, a myth of epic proportions is quite often the end product.

Victoria Wilcox, chairman of the Holliday-Dorsey-Fife House Association of Fayetteville, Georgia, asserts that the "Doc" Holliday of Western lore is in many ways just such a myth.

"I don't think John Henry (Doc) ever wanted to be a gun-fighter," Wilcox asserted in an interview in 1996. "I believe what he really wanted was the kind of life his uncle lived right here in Fayetteville. He was even named after his uncle – Dr. Holliday – who was a medical doctor."

Dr. John Stiles Holliday was the uncle of John Henry "Doc" Holliday of western fame. This artist's rendering of John Stiles was created circa 1860. It was he who diagnosed the tuberculosis in his soon-to-be-famous nephew in 1873. (Collection of Morgan DeLancey Magee)

1

This impressive home built by Dr. John Stiles Holliday in Fayetteville, Georgia, still stands as of this writing. It has been in existence at least since 1855, and quite possibly was built as early as 1846 when Dr. Holliday first purchased the property. It was at this home that young John Henry spent much time in his youth forming a bond with his cousin Mattie which ultimately had a profound impact upon both their lives.

Dr. John Stiles Holliday

Doc's uncle was Dr. John Stiles Holliday, a Fayetteville physician. "John Stiles was the first of the Holliday family to obtain a college degree. John Henry was the second," Ms. Wilcox added, as she quickly ticked off facts about the famed gambler/gunman. Over the years, Wilcox has mentally stockpiled a wealth of information about the Hollidays.

In her capacity with the Holliday-Dorsey-Fife House Association, Ms. Wilcox has made it her business not only to help restore the family home, but the family's legacy as well. And that obviously includes the legacy of John Henry Holliday.

"The Holliday House is the 'most intact' ante-bellum home in all of metro Atlanta," Wilcox noted proudly. "What I mean by intact is that when you walk in, you stand on the original Georgia heart-pine floors that have been there since the house was first built. Very little has been altered in the home since Dr. Holliday first lived here. Plumbing wasn't even added until the 1940s."

The Holliday home, as it exists today, has been around since 1855, but the original structure was probably built even prior to that time, perhaps as early as 1846 when John Stiles Holliday first purchased the property.

"In the vernacular, the original dwelling would have been considered an 'I-frame home,'" explained Wilcox. "A formal entry flanked by two rooms, one on each side with a stairway leading to two more rooms upstairs."

Prior to moving in with his family, Dr. John Stiles Holliday remodeled the house. Without aid of an architect, he added six massive Greek columns to the front verandah. He also added four more rooms to the rear of the home, making a total of four rooms downstairs and four upstairs. And nearby, he cultivated a vegetable garden and a small orchard to provide some of the family's foods.

Famous Connections
The old home has other interesting roots beyond that of the Holliday family. Prior to occupation of the home by his family, Dr. Holliday agreed to allow students at the new Fayetteville Academy to use the then-new home as a boarding house. The Hollidays therefore did not actually take up residence in the home until 1857.

Annie Fitzgerald, the grandmother of famed author Margaret Mitchell (*Gone With The Wind*), was one of the young girls attending Fayetteville Academy. As a result of this family experience, Mitchell would later send her *Gone With The Wind* heroine, "Scarlett O'Hara," to the "Fayetteville Girl's Academy," modeled after Fayetteville Academy.

Mitchell's writings in association with her family experiences did not stop with Scarlett either. Her cousin from the Fitzgerald clan – Martha Anne "Mattie" Holliday – was the prototype for Mitchell's character of "Melanie" in the famed novel.

Mattie spent her childhood in Fayetteville and nearby Jonesboro. The Hollidays were a close-knit Irish clan, and family gatherings at the Holliday home were common.

It was during these and other gatherings that a strong bond between young Mattie and John Henry (Doc) Holliday was established – a relationship about which there has been much speculation and romantic intrigue over the ensuing years.

Cousin Mattie
Only twenty months older than Doc, Mattie Holliday was his playmate and companion during assemblies at the Holliday house in Fayetteville. The secrets the two shared as children formed the basis of an intimacy that lasted throughout their lives. The depth and breadth of this relationship and its exact details are not known today, and perhaps have been lost to posterity, but the subject nevertheless has been fodder for much myth-making over the years.

In the 1993 major motion picture *Tombstone*, starring Kurt Russell and Val Kilmer, a mythical Doc confesses to Wyatt Earp that an affair with a cousin caused her to enter a convent and him to leave his home in disgrace. This, quite possibly, is a very accurate portrayal of the actual circumstances.

Cousin Mattie, born December 14, 1849, was raised a Catholic, and became a nun at the age of 34. She took the name "Melanie" in honor

Martha Anne "Mattie" Holliday was Doc's cousin and his one true love with whom he reportedly had an affair prior to his travels in the West. Martha Anne subsequently joined the Sisters of Mercy convent, changing her name to Sister Mary Melanie. Interestingly, her grandfather – Philip Fitzgerald – was the great-grandfather of Margaret Mitchell who immortalized the Civil War history of Georgia in her best-selling epic, Gone With The Wind. Both the Fitzgerald and Melanie names graced prominent characters in the book. Martha Anne was born December 14, 1849, and died April 19, 1939.

of Saint Melaine, who, after marrying a kinsman, sought a life of complete devotion to God. Did Mattie take the name Melanie because she was in love with her own cousin, Doc?

"Family members in the past have been reluctant to admit that any such relationship actually existed between John Henry and Mattie," confessed Wilcox, "but the myth that he left Georgia simply because of poor health is questionable. John Henry supposedly left Georgia for a higher and dryer climate to combat the tuberculosis with which he had been diagnosed, but he traveled to Dallas, Texas, which is actually a lower elevation, geographically, than even Atlanta, and is almost as humid.

"In all likelihood, the Doc-Mattie relationship probably did in fact play a role in his decision to leave Georgia," Wilcox added. "After all, many people with advanced cases of tuberculosis such as was suffered by Doc were going to Florida for treatment in those days."

In fairness, many travel decisions made by Holliday the last ten or fifteen years of his life were not logical ones, and seem to have been little more than aimless wandering in search of adventure and yet another gambling opportunity. To attach any special significance to his travels from 1873 and later would be pure folly.

Summer Love

It is entirely plausible that Doc fell in love with his favored cousin the year he turned sixteen. In 1864, in an effort to escape the Union army which was advancing into north Georgia, Doc's father had moved the family from Griffin (in north Georgia) to Valdosta (in extreme south Georgia).

After the war, around 1867, Doc spent one summer with Mattie's family in Jonesboro, and it quite possibly was during this period that their romance blossomed. Even long after she became "Sister Melanie," Doc maintained a strong bond with his cousin, often writing to her of secrets only the two of them shared.

Who knows today if these letters and missives were love letters? In point of fact, it will probably never be known now to a certainty. Mattie considered the letters ultra-private, and later burned them to avoid any revelation of the details within them in the future.

According to family legend, Mattie later regretted the destruction of the letters. "Had I not destroyed most of his letters, the world would have known a much different man than the one of Western lore," she later confessed.

According to records, Doc went on to study dentistry at the Pennsylvania College of Dental Surgery, graduating in 1872. He was planning happily for his future, totally unaware he would be gone in a scant fifteen years.

After graduation, Doc practiced dentistry briefly in Atlanta. It was at about this time that he was diagnosed with tuberculosis, a dreaded disease for which there was no cure.

A Move To Dallas

It was shortly after learning of his disease that Doc departed for Texas, quite likely sometime in 1873. One can only imagine the pain and despair his fate must have caused him. He probably had suffered a tragic love affair from which there was no recourse, and then shortly thereafter had been informed that he had contracted a fatal disease.

After arriving in Dallas, Doc must have needed funds, for he set up a dental practice there. At this time, the West was still a wild frontier in many respects. In short order, Doc had become a part of this wildness, picking up the traits of drinking, gambling, and carrying firearms. He, however, also continued to practice dentistry.

According to O.K. Corral chronicler Paula Marks, Doc soon garnered a reputation as "one of the touchiest drunks in the West." Wyatt Earp himself declared "Doc's fatalistic courage... gave (him) the edge over any out-and-out killer I ever knew."

Doc was arrested January 1st, 1875, for shooting at a saloon-keeper in Dallas. According to the January 2, 1875 issue of the *Dallas Herald*, "Dr. Holliday and Mr. Austin, a saloon keeper, relieved the monotony of the noise of fire crackers by taking a couple of shots at each other yesterday afternoon. The cheerful note of the peaceful six-shooter is heard once more among us. Both shooters were arrested."

Doc apparently decided at that point that it was time to leave Dallas, and drifted on to Fort Griffin. There, he was indicted by a grand jury for "gaming in a saloon," along with Hurricane Bill, Liz, Etta, Kate, et alle, and charged with keeping a "disorderly house."

"Kate," "Bat," and Wyatt

This "Kate" named in the indictment was the first published link between Doc and the female who eventually became known in Western lore as "Big Nose Kate." Along with Doc, Mary Katherine "Kate" Harony would become widely known for her "adventures."

From 1875 to 1878, little is accurately known about Doc's wanderings. It is known, however, that he eventually traveled with Kate to Denver, Colorado, where he began dealing a popular card game called faro.

By late 1877, Doc and Kate were back in Fort Griffin. It was here that he first met another drifter who would gain fame in the West by the name of Wyatt Earp. Doc's illness and frail health no doubt caused him to prefer New Mexico, Texas, Kansas and Arizona in the winter months, saving the gambling opportunities in the gold and silver mining towns in Colorado and parts northward for the summer months.

By 1878, Doc had arrived in Dodge City, already preceded by a rather substantial reputation as a dangerous man. It was here that he played poker in the Long Branch Saloon, and rode in posses with Wyatt Earp and Bat Masterson. Masterson, who disliked Doc and later became a writer of sorts, penned a number of articles – after Doc's death – which portrayed the Georgian in a negative light.

According to an article Masterson wrote in a 1907 issue of *Human Life* magazine, Doc "went from Dodge to Trinidad, Colorado, where, within a week from the time he landed, he shot and seriously wounded a young sport by the name of Kid Colton over a very trivial matter. He was again forced to hunt the tall timber and managed to make his escape to Las Vegas, New Mexico, which was then something of a boom town..."

Masterson later wrote that "Holliday had few friends anywhere in the West. He was selfish and had a perverse nature–traits not calculated to make a man popular in the early days on the frontier."

Whatever the circumstances, the John Henry Holliday described by William Barclay "Bat" Masterson did not match the description of the Southern gentleman of record back in Georgia. But who was "Bat" Masterson anyway?

Uncovering The Myth...
And His Griffin, Georgia, Home

Recent investigations and research on John Henry Holliday have revealed some captivating details, particularly as concerns his former homes in Griffin, Georgia.

Bill Dunn is a man on a mission. A distant cousin to Griffin native John Henry "Doc" Holliday, Dunn has made it his goal in life to get the truth out about his famous forebear, to see the "real" Doc Holliday – the Southern gentleman as opposed to the reckless outlaw – presented for posterity.

As simple as that might seem, it, in fact, is considerably difficult to achieve, especially when dealing with a Western legend whose fascinating life has inspired multiple interpretations.

Dunn, however, must have luck on his side. Since he began researching his famous relative in the 1980s, he has managed to uncover quite a bit of previously unknown information pertaining to the dentist-gambler and his Griffin roots.

Bill Dunn, a distant cousin to Doc Holliday, rests his foot on a fieldstone believed to have been part of the foundation of the famous gunman's boyhood home in Griffin. Holliday lived here from age 2 to age 12. (Photo by Jackie Kennedy)

For instance, Dunn has discovered evidence that Doc actually practiced dentistry in Griffin – a detail heretofore unsubstantiated. He also has researched two "Holliday" graves in the local cemetery believed to be those of Doc's father's slaves, and two other graves in the same cemetery which he maintains are "more than likely" those of Doc and his equally-elusive father.

This property at the corner of Tinsley and North 9th streets in Griffin was owned by Doc Holliday's father, Major Henry B. Holliday, and undoubtedly was the site of the Holliday home in which Doc lived until he was two years of age. (Photo by Jackie Kennedy)

Most recently, Dunn and fellow Doc enthusiasts discovered the actual site upon which Holliday's plantation home in Griffin once stood. "This find," says Dunn, "is the most satisfying of all. While the other discoveries happened along the way, this is the one I've been pursuing for two decades."

Hitting The Jackpot

John Henry was born Aug. 14, 1851, in Griffin, a west-central Georgia town with a population of 22,000 at the dawning of the 21st century. He was the only living child of Henry Burroughs and Alice Jane McKey Holliday. Prior to his birth, a sister, Martha Eleanora, had died at the age of six months.

John Henry was born in a house which once stood at the corner of what today is Tinsley and North 9th Street, according to Dunn. A modest brick residence – the nicest house in this lower income neighborhood – now occupies this corner lot. The current residents of this home quite possibly have no clue today that they live on ground once occupied by a Western legend.

John Henry's father had served in both the Indian and Mexican wars by the time his only son was born. Ten years later, the elder Holliday joined the Confederate Army and fought in his third war.

During the decade in-between these two wars, Henry Burroughs had worked as a druggist in Griffin and served as the first elected clerk of court there. His family – though not wealthy – was stable and socially prominent. They attended Griffin's First Presbyterian Church where records today indicate the infant John Henry Holliday was baptized at the age of seven months in 1852.

When John Henry was two years old, the family moved to a 148-acre plantation in rural Griffin. It is the location of this homestead that had eluded historians in the 20th century, and that Dunn had long hoped to find.

"I'd been looking for twenty years," he said. "I'd get close but just couldn't pinpoint the location." Destiny, however, walked through his door a year ago, and Dunn said he still gets goose bumps talking about it.

An employee of Spring Industries – which owns the former Holliday plantation property – had been researching water locations at the site when he reportedly came across a copy of a 140-year-old map. "Bill, I think you'll be interested in this," the worker said as he conversed with him that day.

To his amazement, Dunn discovered the map described in detail the lay of the land of "Camp Stephens," a Griffin-based Confederate Army camp which existed in 1862. Major Henry Burroughs Holliday had sold 136 of his original 147 acres to the Confederate Army for construction of the camp, leaving 11 acres for his family's residence. There, on the map, was clearly listed "H.B. Holliday's second home." Confederate Private Asbury H. Jackson had given the original map to Doc's mother in March of 1862.

"You search for something for years, then somebody just walks in and hands it to you," Dunn smiled, still incredulous. To top things off, the fellow who presented him the prized map was a man who had somewhat irritated him the year before at "Doc Holliday Days," an annual event in Griffin.

"Camp Stephens," a Griffin-based Confederate Army camp which existed in 1862. Major Henry Burroughs Holliday had sold 136 of his original 147 acres to the Confederate Army for construction of the camp, leaving 11 acres for his family's residence.

9

Henry Burroughs Holliday, Doc's father, was photographed circa 1852, while the family yet lived in Griffin, Georgia, south of Atlanta.

"This newspaperman asked me about Doc and I pointed him to several experts who were attending the event," Dunn explained. "Instead of interviewing them, he goes up to this fellow (the eventual map-bearer) who had a tattoo of Doc above his ankle. He asked the guy, 'How do you feel about having someone who drank too much, gambled and killed people depicted on your body?'

"Instead of defending Doc, this fellow responded, 'It don't bother me. I do a little of that myself, except for the killing.' Needless to say, I was a little perturbed with him," Dunn confided.

Keeping his frustration to himself, Dunn said his resolve paid dividends in the end when the tattooed fellow presented him with the map in the summer of 2002.

Walking Hallowed Ground

The map had barely exchanged hands when Dunn solicited help from two friends – fellow members of the Doc Holliday Society (of which he serves as president) – who were in town that August weekend for Doc's annual birthday bash.

With Gene Carlisle, a Holliday researcher who has penned a manuscript on the Western legend, Dunn set out hiking. Using the map as their guide, the men followed the old Macon and Western Railroad line toward the house site, battling tree branches, vines and undergrowth as they searched for the site of the old home-place.

Veering off the historic railroad tracks, the men cut their way through one particularly dense area of undergrowth for a short distance before stumbling upon a scattered pile of ancient fieldstones which the men now believe were used in the foundation of the Holliday house.

"Gene," Dunn uttered, barely able to breathe. "I think we've found it."

The next day, Keith Reed – Holliday Society member and the third explorer – entered the wooded area himself at a different angle, hoping to prove Dunn's assumption correct.

"He said he was practically eaten alive by redbugs," Dunn smiled, "but he stepped off the map's directives and landed on the exact same spot, confirming it as the former Holliday home-place."

The site is about two miles from Griffin's town square. Interestingly, Dunn says some earthworks from Camp Stephens – just as they appeared during the Civil War – remain in the vicinity adjacent to the home-site.

As the war worsened for the South in 1864 – and with the Confederate camp barely a hop, skip and jump from the Holliday home – it does not take a rocket scientist to understand

John Henry Holliday from a tinted daguerreotype, 1852. (from the collection of Karen Holliday Tanner)

why Major Holliday moved his family to Bemiss (a south Georgia town near Valdosta) that same year, almost simultaneously as William T. Sherman's Army was marching toward middle Georgia.

"Surely," said Dunn, "the major (medically discharged in 1862 due to 'watery dysentery') reckoned Sherman would march right by his home with destruction in mind. Seeking safety, he undoubtedly moved his family farther southward, eventually settling in Valdosta where he acquired more than 2,000 acres and ultimately served four terms as the city's mayor."

John Henry's Georgia

Back in Griffin, Georgia, tangible reminders of Doc's days in this town are abundant even today if one knows where to look. Bill Dunn happily points these out to curious visitors to his town today.

There is John Henry's birthplace on Tinsley Street and the Holliday plantation. There's the former site of First Presbyterian Church where he was baptized. (The Griffin Fire Station stands on this site today.) There's the old Iron Front Building which he once owned and in which he is believed to have practiced dentistry. There also is the old courthouse in Griffin where Major Holliday served as clerk of court. And at Oak Hill Cemetery, there's the final resting place of Doc's sister – and possibly other graves of even more importance.

11

A bit beyond John Henry's sister's grave are the graves of Mariah and Harry Holliday, a black couple who, according to Dunn, probably were slaves on the Holliday plantation.

"By all indications," said Dunn, "the Hollidays were good and decent people who cared for their workers." Despite a common tendency to believe that hatred and violence sparked all relationships between whites and blacks of the pre-Civil War era, Dunn – just as other Southern historians – asserts that nothing could be further from the truth. He said this was particularly true in regard to the Holliday family.

"Doc, in fact, probably even picked up his card-playing skills from a slave girl – Sophie Walton"–Dunn continued, "with whom he often played as a child. She resided at his Uncle John Holliday's farm. According to family tradition, it was Sophie who taught a young John Henry the skills he later used to support himself as a gambler after tuberculosis robbed him of the ability to practice dentistry. She reportedly taught him a number of the tricks of the trade, such as 'skinning' cards and 'the put-and-take' technique of dealing cards."

Doc, the Dentist

One of the most intriguing "Doc sites" in Griffin is the building where he may have practiced dentistry after leaving the practice at which he was working in Atlanta. In a 1940 *Griffin Daily News* article, Judge L.P. Goodrich noted that his father had known the Hollidays. The article goes on to state, "Doc Holliday returned to Griffin after the war and practiced dentistry here in an office in the old Merritt building."

It is a matter of public record that John Henry, in fact, once was part owner of the Merritt building, known in the 1870s as the Iron Front building. He had inherited half of the property from his mother's estate, and her family – the McKeys – had claimed the other half.

"They actually drew a line down the middle of the building, separating the two halves," Dunn added. "Doc later sold his half for $1,800.00, which was a good price for that property back then."

Dunn said he feels certain Doc practiced dentistry in an upstairs office at the Iron Front. After graduating from Valdosta Institute in 1870, Doc had entered the Pennsylvania College of Dental Surgery from which he was graduated in 1872.

He subsequently returned south and worked for Dr. Arthur C. Ford in his dental practice in Atlanta, while living with his Uncle John Stiles Holliday a short distance away. While Ford attended the Southern Dental Association Conference in Richmond, Virginia, in the summer of

The petite grave of Martha Eleanora Holliday, Doc Holliday's infant sister who died at the age of six months, is located at Oak Hill Cemetery in Griffin. She died in 1850, the year before her famous brother was born. (Photo by Jackie Kennedy)

1872, Dr. John Henry Holliday was left in charge of Ford's practice. When the elder dentist returned, Holliday was left with time on his hands – time to commute to Griffin to operate his own dental practice, said Dunn.

"If he practiced here, this is where he did it," Dunn said, pointing to four holes in the original wooden floor situated in strategic spots to accommodate a dental chair of that time period. Equally interesting is a tin cylinder discovered under a loose floor plank in this same upstairs room at Holliday's Portions & Elixirs, a restaurant that now occupied the old Iron Front building as of this writing.

"He probably used this for dental supplies or to hide money in," said Dunn who researched the cylinder, stamped *Great Northern Manufacturing Company, Chicago*, and found it to be of Civil War-era vintage. *Great Northern* did, indeed, carry dental supplies too.

"It sure does lend credence to the possibility that Doc practiced dentistry here for two or three months before heading out West," Dunn concluded.

Resting In Peace, But Where?

While history claims that Doc Holliday is buried in Glenwood Springs, Colorado, persistent rumors through the years have alluded that Major Henry B. Holliday in fact brought his son's body back to Georgia for burial. It's one rumor in which Dunn places some credence.

"Yes, I sincerely believe that," he stated emphatically. "Knowing Southern history as I do – and knowing the major had the motive, the money, the mode of transportation, and nothing to stop him – I believe he brought Doc back and buried him under this oak tree," Dunn said, pointing to a stately oak in Griffin's Oak Hill Cemetery. "Until someone proves otherwise to me, I'll believe Doc's buried right here beside the major."

An infant John Henry Holliday–his painful future worlds away–was photographed with his mother, Alice Jane McKey Holliday circa 1852. Even as a small tyke, John Henry demonstrates a gaze which might be unsettling to some. (Craig Fouts Photo Collection)

The unmarked twin graves at Oak Hill are compelling. Set off to themselves, they are covered by unassuming concrete slabs with no engravings. Dunn theorizes that Major Holliday either went to Colorado himself or sent a relative to retrieve his son's remains, then buried his boy under the now-massive oak.

Interestingly, a heavy-duty ancient nail is driven, rock-solid, into a sprawling root of the oak, centered above what Dunn believes to be Doc's grave. Dunn conjectures the major quite possibly could have hammered in the nail and used it to work a pulley to lower his son's casket into its final resting place.

"The nail-pulley mechanism would have enabled him to accomplish the two-man job on his own," said Dunn. It's a plausible theory if you believe the major wanted his boy's gravesite to be kept a secret.

Supporting his belief that father and son are buried in Griffin are these notes of interest: 1) While Doc is said to be buried at Glenwood Springs, Colorado, the marker in the cemetery there reads, "This memorial dedicated to Doc Holliday who is buried 'someplace' in this cemetery." It is a fact that no one today knows the actual gravesite in Glenwood Springs, containing Holliday's last remains. 2) While some Valdostans believe Major Henry Burroughs Holliday is buried in that Georgia town, no one knows the exact location of his gravesite either. Dunn finds it difficult to believe that the grave of a man of his prominence (veteran of three wars and a four-term mayor) would be unknown and unmarked today if indeed it did exist in Valdosta. 3) The twin graves in Griffin are in the Thomas family plot. Dunn said the Thomas and Holliday families were socially connected and the Thomases may very well have acceded to Major Holliday's request and agreed to the anonymous burial of Doc Holliday in their plot.

"Why can't the folks in Glenwood Springs point to Doc's grave?" questioned Dunn. "It's because it's not there. Major Holliday had the motive and the means to bring his boy back to Griffin. A man of Southern heritage would want his son buried near him, and removing him to an anonymous location would prevent the vandalism that surely would have followed had Doc's gravesite been revealed."

Major Henry Holliday, Doc's father, was the first clerk of court in Spalding County. The historic courthouse, which still stands downtown, included an office for Holliday in the 1850s. (Photo by Jackie Kennedy)

Gentleman From Georgia

They say you can take the boy out of Georgia but can't take Georgia out of the boy. John Henry Holliday left the South and lived as Doc Holliday his last 15 years out West. But did he long for home?

An 1882 *Atlanta Constitution* interview with Holliday family friend Lee Smith indicates he did. When asked if Doc ever spoke of returning to Georgia, Smith responded, "He would be back here today but for fear of being handed over to the Arizona authorities."

By the 1880s, however, the West had claimed Doc Holliday as its own. He ultimately died in a Colorado hotel on Nov. 8, 1887, tuberculosis finally defeating him.

It's a matter of public record that John Henry died out West, but, if Bill Dunn's theory about the two graves at Oak Hill Cemetery in Griffin, Georgia is correct, the noted gunman did, indeed, come home to Georgia a final time.

Bill Dunn said he likes Tombstone (Arizona) Historian Ben Traywick's description of Doc Holliday best: "He was an orchid in a cactus patch."

Several years ago, Dunn received a call from Traywick when the Tombstone historian was working on his book, *John Henry: The Doc Holliday Story*.

"He asked me to help and I asked him how he intended to portray Doc," Dunn recalled. Traywick replied, "As the true Southern, educated gentleman that he was."

15

Sophie Walton was a female slave born in January of 1856 on a farm owned by the Walton family. Sophie enjoyed a higher status than the other slave children because she had been fathered by Mr. Walton. During the Federal occupation of Georgia, Mr. Walton could no longer care for all his slaves, and arranged for Sophie to go to the home of Dr. John Stiles Holliday, Doc's uncle. Among her many skills, Sophie was extremely adept at cards, and taught Doc the skills he later used as a professional card player out West. Sophie was photographed here in 1895 in Atlanta, Georgia.

"What can I do to help?" Dunn said he responded. Published in 1996, the book, to Dunn's delight, "does nothing to discredit Doc."

Known best for teaming with the Earp brothers to defeat the Clantons and McLaurys in the 1881 gunfight near the O.K. Corral, Doc Holliday became a larger-than-life legend. Over the next century, stories of him would range from fact to fabrication with his reputation as a ruthless gunman dominating. Numerous publications and Hollywood movies would paint the picture of a merciless killer with murder in his heart.

The facts, said Dunn, paint a different picture – that of an educated gentleman who never abandoned his Southern roots. Either way, the intrigue of Doc Holliday continues, even as it did a century ago.

"This guy from Buckhead, Georgia called to get information for a report his 11-year-old daughter was doing on Doc," said Dunn. "He said she was infatuated with him and that after seeing the movie *Tombstone*, she could recite all of actor Val Kilmer's dialogue in the movie."

While some insist on portraying John Henry as a killer without a conscience, Dunn vows the dentist from Griffin fired a weapon only when he had to, and he never became comfortable with killing. The handsome ash-blond, blue-eyed Georgian who departed his home for the drier climate out West to slow the stranglehold of tuberculosis was most likely "a very typical young guy, mischievous with an out-going personality," says Dunn.

A Move To Valdosta

His legacy as a gambler and fearsome gunfighter in the old West are secure. Lesser known, however, are the details of John Henry's life during his adolescence in Valdosta, Georgia.

I f there is one sure thing that can be said of the legacy of Doc Holliday, it is that there is virtually no agreement whatsoever about many aspects of his life.

No one knows this better than Susan McKey Thomas of Valdosta, Georgia, the legendary gunfighter's first cousin once removed, who spent the better part of three decades trying to sort through competing popular mythologies for the truth.

"I have no ax to grind, and I have no one to protect," said Thomas in an interview in 1999. Her sharp wit and elegantly groomed appearance offered only a little hint of her age. "I'm just trying to get to the truth."

Thomas's historical odyssey began in 1972, when members of the Lowndes County Historical Society were asked to submit summaries of their family backgrounds for inclusion in the society's records.

The Holliday home in Valdosta, where a young John Henry spent his adolescence attending Valdosta Institute and hunting and fishing in the countryside.

Wading into waters fraught with hearsay and legend, Thomas and Albert Pendleton, secretary of the society's newsletter, discovered what Thomas called "many shocking inaccuracies" about her famous relative.

Research Discoveries

"One of the first things we found out was that Wyatt Earp was little more than a pimp," explained Pendleton. Indeed, historians support the claim that several of the Earp brothers and their wives – some of whom were prostitutes themselves – ran brothels across the Old West.

The story of Doc Holliday in the West, however accurate it may or may not be, is reasonably well-known. Less known, however, is the story of the Holliday family in Valdosta, where John Henry spent much of his adolescence.

Even here, Thomas and Pendleton ran into a myriad of conflicting stories, enough so that it took 18 months of painstaking research before Thomas felt she could submit her family story to the historical society.

The work of Thomas and Pendleton, in fact, turned up so much information that Thomas's contribution took the form of a book, *In Search of the Hollidays*, published in 1973 by Little River Press. "We found out so many things that it just seemed like we needed to write them down," Pendleton said.

The book turned out to be something of a local sensation, and in the years that followed, copies were sold to history buffs from almost every state and several foreign countries. From that effort, the desire to know more about her famous forebear drove Thomas to an ongoing investigation of much of the Holliday mystique, including the eight years in which John Henry lived in Valdosta.

Early Valdosta Days

The story of John Henry Holliday in Valdosta begins early in 1864, when his father, Major Henry Burroughs Holliday, brought his family to a settlement of about 1,500 people in what then was a virtual wilderness in extreme south Georgia. It was far from the Holliday family home in Griffin, Georgia, but it was a safe haven from the looming Federal siege of Atlanta and the advancing Yankees.

Major Holliday, a veteran of the Creek Indian wars, the Mexican War and the Civil War, had retired from military service and found refuge in a large tract of land northeast of Valdosta, near a tiny community known as Bemiss.

By that time, the Hollidays had already reared to manhood a young orphan – Francisco Hidalgo – brought home by Major Holliday in 1849

John Henry Holliday was photographed here shortly after his graduation from the Pennsylvania College of Dental Surgery. He lived a scant 15 years after this photo was taken, the last few months of which were spent in Leadville and Glenwood Springs, Colorado. (Photo by O.B. DeMorat)

after the Mexican War.

In earlier years when he had lived in Griffin, Georgia, Major Holliday – as he was formally known – had worked as a druggist. In the largely unsettled south Georgia countryside, however, he became an entrepreneur, opening a plant nursery, planting vineyards and promoting the production of pecans, a profession which has grown into a major agricultural industry today stretching from Valdosta westward across the clay hills of southwest Georgia.

Ms. Thomas said the young John Holliday, 12 years old when he arrived in Valdosta, was remembered by area residents as being nice looking and slightly built, with piercing blue eyes and blonde hair.

Later biographies recorded Doc Holliday's gracious manners as well as his unpredictable temperament, but Valdostans remembered only a well-mannered adolescent who dressed neatly and grew into a young man known for his ability on a dance floor amidst the musical talent of his McKey relatives.

The McKey Family

History correctly records that young John Henry was well-educated. He was schooled at the private Valdosta Institute which, as reported by Louis Pendleton in his *Echo of Drums*, stressed classics and taught "advanced branches." Headmaster Samuel McWhir Varnedoe set up a challenging curriculum including Greek, Latin, French, advanced English, mathematics and history.

Following the end of the Civil War, the Holliday/McKey family clung to at least an appearance of affluence. The young Holliday's three McKey uncles, James, William and Thomas, bought a large tract of land in the lakes area along the Georgia-Florida border south of Valdosta in an area known as Bellview.

The McKey property, known as Banner Plantation, is said to have been a favorite haunt of John Henry, who reportedly spent much of his adolescent years hunting and fishing on the property. His favorite uncle, Tom, who was only 10 years older than John, often accompanied him.

Years later and a world away out West, John Henry assumed the alias Thomas "Mackey" (as the family surname was then spelled) for a short time, presumably because he had encountered legal problems or conflicts of another nature, and needed to disguise his identity.

"I don't know why he did that," Thomas said in her 1999 interview. "He wasn't famous, really, until the O.K. Corral."

Many historians would reply, however, that despite the fact that he hadn't yet been involved in the famous gunfight in Tombstone, John Henry was, nevertheless, becoming known as a testy gunfighter even by the time he reached Dodge City.

Whatever the case, back in south Georgia, what seems to have been an idyllic childhood for John Henry was shattered by tragedy in the form of the unexpected serious illness of his mother. Alice Jane McKey Holliday gradually lost her strength and endured a lingering and torturous state of health until September 16, 1866, when she finally passed away. John Henry, who had dearly loved his mother, reportedly was devastated.

As if his mother's death was not bad enough, family stories, maintain that John Henry was shaken even worse by the remarriage of his father a mere three months after his mother's death. Major Holliday married Rachel Martin, 23, a young lady who was less than half his age and only nine years older than John Henry.

Reconstruction Trauma

Other outside factors also impacted the Holliday family in Valdosta. Following the U.S. Civil War, the turbulent years of Reconstruction took a serious toll on the Holliday family's financial fortunes.

Rachel Martin's family owned farmland which adjoined the Holliday property. Records indicate that the Martins purchased the Holliday tract, and that Major Holliday's father-in-law gave to his daughter a house in Valdosta at 405 Savannah Avenue. The Holliday family – including young John Henry – soon relocated to this new address.

Never one to take defeat easily, Major Holliday immediately began working to recover the family fortune. He opened several businesses, including a furniture store. The 1870 Census lists him broadly as "general agent." Eventually, Thomas says, Holliday regained all of his former properties.

Major Holliday also gained some acclaim in the political arena in his community. He served four terms as Valdosta's mayor.

However, while his father was prospering, the younger Holliday began pursuing the behavior for which he would become more widely known later in life. Local tradition maintains that he eventually fled town after running afoul of law enforcement officials, although the specifics of his misdeeds are not clear today.

Clues can be found in what has been called a "racially-motivated" shooting incident (much of which has been debunked today) in which the teenaged Holliday reportedly was involved. He was also accused of being associated with – and indeed may even have been the mastermind of – a plot to destroy with explosives the federally-operated Lowndes County Courthouse.

Swimming Hole Incident

Ms. Thomas said she can confirm that the young Holliday was indeed involved in a shooting incident reportedly prompted by his discovery of either a black man or a group of blacks in a swimming hole normally used by whites near the confluence of the Withlacoochee and Little rivers at the old settlement of Troupville.

This incident also occurred during the Reconstruction years, when racial tensions were high. At that time, many blacks reveled in their new-found status, often intentionally inflaming a situation by flaunting their ability to violate long-standing Southern social mores.

Ms. Thomas said the story involving John Henry was confirmed by none other than Thomas McKey, John's uncle and source of the alias John Henry later used out West. In the late 1920s, Thomas says McKey related the incident involving John Henry to writer Stuart Lake who was working on what later would become a controversial book about Wyatt Earp.

"He told the story of (McKey and Holliday) going to a swimming hole where whites swam, and they found some blacks in the water," Ms. Thomas related. "[John Henry] first ordered the blacks out, and then he turned to get his pistol... but one of the blacks got out a gun when he saw that Doc had turned to get his gun."

According to local tradition, a black federal officer was killed in the incident, but in the interview with writer Stuart Lake, Thomas McKey firmly denied anyone was even wounded by a bullet.

Today, there is no microfilm available for the *Valdosta Times* newspaper during the period in question, but McKey's assertion of John Henry's innocence is given some credence by the fact that there is no evidence of

Valdosta Institute, a private school, provided young John Henry with an education in the classics. The date of this photo is unknown, but it quite likely was taken circa 1870s.

such an incident in the records of the superior court for the years 1866 through 1873.

A newspaper account of the plan to destroy the courthouse has been discovered, but it does not implicate John Henry. It does, however, give the name of five other individuals who were accused of the crime.

Major Holliday was one of five men appointed by the Valdosta City Council to draw up a plan to deal with the unrest in the area during Reconstruction according to Ms. Thomas. One could surmise that John Henry's family connections could have protected him from prosecution in the courthouse incident, but any such conclusion, like so many others involving Doc Holliday, would be pure conjecture at this late date.

On To Dental School

Despite the trouble John Henry may have initiated as a teen, he went on to graduate from the Valdosta Institute in 1870. Later that year, he applied and was admitted to the Pennsylvania College of Dental Surgery from which he was graduated during the 16th annual graduation ceremonies on March 1, 1872.

During his studies in Pennsylvania, John Henry occasionally returned to work his required "preceptership" with Valdosta dentist Lucian Frederick Frink. Ms. Thomas said there is some evidence that Holliday performed dental work in Valdosta in October of 1871, and it is believed he returned home for a brief visit after his graduation, but a short time later, he struck out for Atlanta to open a dental practice in that newly-rebuilt city.

Though he did not know it at the time, even as he left Valdosta, the newly anointed "Dr." Holliday was no doubt already a doomed man. Within a year, he would be diagnosed with tuberculosis, a disease for which there was no treatment until the mid-20th century.

Historians and researchers today maintain that John Henry almost certainly had been infected with the tuberculosis bacterium years prior to the diagnosis of his disease. He might possibly have contracted it from a dental patient upon which he trained early in his college education. He may also have been infected by his mother, whose death in 1866, in fact, is believed to have been from TB, although Thomas says there is no proof of that today.

Interestingly, Francisco Hidalgo, the Mexican youth raised by the Hollidays is known to have died of the dreaded disease as well in 1873, providing still more strong evidence that the seeds of Doc Holliday's eventual demise in a Colorado hotel in 1887 were sown long before that time, either in Griffin or in Valdosta.

Leaving Home Forever

Once he left Valdosta, Doc Holliday apparently considered his break with south Georgia to be permanent. There is no evidence that he ever returned to visit.

A legend within the Holliday family maintains that Major

During his service for the United States in the Mexican War, Henry Burroughs Holliday brought home a young Mexican orphan–Francisco Hidalgo– and raised him to maturity in the Holliday home. On June 12, 1854, Francisco married Martha Freeman in Butts Co., Georgia. Interestingly, he died of tuberculosis on January 13, 1873, fourteen years prior to the death of his famous step-brother, John Henry Holliday. Was he the source of the terrible disease that killed Doc?

Holliday arranged a meeting with his son while in New Orleans at a Confederate veterans' convention in 1885, and begged the ailing Doc to come home to his family. Whether the meeting ever took place or not is, predictably, unverifiable today.

What can be said with certainty, however, is that if the estranged father and son had such a meeting, it was their last. Doc Holliday did not return to Georgia, and by 1885, he was so sick that he could barely manage to support himself in the gambling profession any longer.

During her research of John Henry Holliday, Susan Thomas did make one very interesting – and very unexpected – discovery. The orphan – Francisco Hidalgo – left behind a legacy of his own in neighboring Berrien County in the form of the "Edalgo" family, of which he was the progenitor.

After more than a century, that piece of information came as a complete and total surprise to the Edalgos who continue to live in this south Georgia county even as of this writing, and who previously had been unable to trace their ancestry beyond their local community.

Remnants In Valdosta

Today, the Holliday legacy is alive and well in Valdosta, even if the Major and Doc are long gone and the Holliday name itself has all but disappeared in the community.

Major Holliday, in addition to serving as mayor of the city, rose to additional prominence in that town. He served as secretary of the Lowndes County Agricultural Society, secretary of the Confederate Veterans of Camp Troup, census enumerator, and superintendent of local elections. He even had a street named for him near the original site of the Holliday house off Savannah Avenue.

The Holliday house in Valdosta – John Henry's adolescent home – lives on as well as of this writing. In the 1970s, the aged structure was purchased by Valdosta businessman Dick Davis and moved to a new location off U.S. Highway 41 South. A few years later, the home was given a new lease on life when it was purchased by a local couple and moved to one of the new subdivisions which sprawl far to the northwest of town.

After its relocation, the house was extensively renovated, although many of its original aspects were preserved and incorporated into the new additions to the structure. As of this writing, it is owned and occupied by Dr. David Johnson and his wife, Susan, at 2605 Pebblewood Drive in Valdosta.

The Iron Front Building

It has stood in this middle Georgia town since the days of the Wild West. Indeed, it once was co-owned by one of the most famed old West icons of all time.

Dallas, Deadwood, Dodge City, Tombstone... the names evoke images of the wild, wild West and the legendary world of John Henry Holliday. Doc, however, had another world as well – a Southern world that still remains in Georgia landmarks like the Holliday House in Fayetteville, Georgia, the former Holliday home in Valdosta, Georgia, and the Griffin, Georgia office building where a young Dr. John H. Holliday once reportedly practiced dentistry prior to the diagnosis of his ill health.

The Iron Front Building on Griffin's historic Solomon Street was a portion of John Henry's inheritance from his mother, Alice Jane McKey Holliday. When Alice Jane died in 1867, the building was passed to thir-

Holliday's Portions & Elixirs on Solomon Street occupies the lower level of the downtown Griffin building once owned by Doc Holliday. He inherited this building from his mother's estate upon her death, and had set up a dental practice here in the summer of 1872. It was at this same time that he learned he had contracted tuberculosis. (Photo by Jackie Kennedy)

teen-year-old John, with his father, Henry Burroughs Holliday acting as his guardian over the property.

A short three months later, Henry Burroughs shocked the Holliday family by quickly remarrying. The rift which resulted in the family is understandable, but it also surprisingly caused John Henry's relatives on his mother's side to sue him to reclaim Alice Jane's property.

The suit, interestingly, was brought by John Henry's (Doc's) uncle, Tom McKey, and was tried in the Lowndes County courthouse in Valdosta. Ironically, this is the same uncle who Doc so admired, and whose name Doc later used as an alias to disguise his own identity while in Colorado. Even more surprising is the fact that the case, *McKey vs Holliday*, ultimately was decided at least partially in favor of the McKey family, causing Alice Jane's estate to be divided equally between the McKeys and John Henry.

In deciding this case, the judge decreed that the building would be divided – literally – by a partition right down the middle, with the eastern half to be returned to McKey ownership and the western half to remain as John Henry's inheritance. Though this case and decision obviously denied John Henry a substantial portion of his "legal" inheritance, history does not record his reaction to the decision or to his McKey relatives who prevailed in the case.

The Iron Front was certainly a property worth fighting for. It was an impressive structure, two stories high with an iron infrastructure beneath its fancy red brick façade. Both floors of the building had long multi-paned windows facing the street in Doc's day. They allowed the morning sunlight to stream into the rooms with their hardwood floors and pressed-tin trimmed ceilings.

At the rear of the main floor, a huge mechanical lift carried merchandise from the loading dock to the second floor sales offices. In Doc's day, the Iron Front was leased out as shop space to various businesses, and brought in good income in rents.

Henry Burroughs Holliday continued his guardianship of the property until his son reached the age of 21 in the summer of 1872 and obtained his inheritance. At that time, John Henry had just graduated from dental school in Philadelphia, and was working in the Atlanta dental office of Dr. Arthur C. Ford on Alabama Street in the vicinity of the present-day complex known as "Underground Atlanta."

With his own office building, John Henry enjoyed the unique distinction of being able to immediately open his own practice in a distinguished building in his old hometown of Griffin. It is believed today that he in fact did return to Griffin and open a small practice there for a brief time.

John Henry registered his ownership of the Iron Front Building in the Spalding County Deed Book in November of 1872. According to old-time Griffin residents, he also did a little remodeling to the building, adding an iron staircase which rose from the alley beside the building up to the little second floor office where he set up his practice.

Dr. John Henry Holliday's shingle, however, didn't hang in Griffin very long. In January of 1873, he sold his half of the Iron Front Building, and by October of that year, records indicate he was practicing dentistry in far-away Dallas, Texas – the

Tiffany Hinton, a waitress at Holliday's Portions & Elixirs, lifts a section of loose plank from the floor of the office where Doc Holliday is believed to have briefly practiced dentistry in Griffin. When she first discovered the hiding spot, Tiffany found a tin cylinder inside, a Civil War-era item produced by a company which manufactured dental supplies. The hiding spot undoubtedly was used by a dentist in yesteryear, possibly even by Holliday himself. In front of this open space in the foreground, a drilled hole is visible. It is one of four such holes into which a dental chair of the 1870s was fitted. (Photo by Jackie Kennedy)

first stop "Doc" made in his western wanderings.

What was it that made John Henry leave Georgia so abruptly after starting his dental practice, selling his hard-won inheritance and traveling west? Some say it was the tuberculosis with which he had been diagnosed by his uncle, Dr. John Stiles Holliday earlier that year. Others claim it was a star-crossed romance with his cousin, Mattie Holliday (daughter of Dr. John Stiles) from which Doc was running.

Whatever the circumstances, vestiges and memories of Doc Holliday remain strong in his Georgia homeland. And visitors to the little second-floor office in Griffin's Iron Front Building constantly imagine what it was like in the days of yesteryear, when a fearless Western gunfighter was a simple dentist in a sleepy Southern town.

Travels In The West

A native son of the old South, Doc Holliday earned lasting fame in the old West in the 1880s.

John Henry traveled to and took up temporary residence in many towns of the old West. Places such as Dallas, Fort Griffin and Jacksboro, Texas; Pueblo, Gunnison, Leadville, Glenwood Springs and Denver, Colorado; Cheyenne, Wyoming; Deadwood, South Dakota (He reportedly was there when his friend, James Butler Hickok, was murdered); Dodge City, Kansas; Las Vegas, New Mexico; Prescott, and Tucson, Arizona, and numerous others all witnessed the comings and goings of Doc. However, it was the town of Tombstone that truly defined him. It was the years he spent in Tombstone – while he was still reasonably healthy – that gave him lasting fame.

By the early 1990s – with the Hollywood releases of movies such as *Tombstone* (1993) starring Val Kilmer, Kurt Russell, and Sam Elliott – the name "Doc" Holliday had reached almost mythic proportions in the folklore of America, but it was not always so. After the initial newspaper

The Dodge House - When John Henry arrived in Dodge City sometime around 1878, this is the rooming house in which he stayed. It was a rough and tumble town full of cattle drovers and other hard-nosed drifters, some of whom occasionally challenged Holliday until his reputation began preceding him.

The Longbranch Saloon in Dodge City was nowhere near as impressive as the descriptions passed down in folklore and the impressions made by television westerns. Nevertheless, it was here that Doc, the Earps, Bat Masterson, Bill Tilghman and many other notables from the history of the old West passed many hours drinking, gambling and carousing in this former cowtown. (Courtesy of Kansas State Historical Society, Topeka, Kansas)

coverage of the shoot-out at the O.K. Corral in Tombstone in October of 1881, much of the fame of Wyatt Earp; his brothers Virgil, Morgan and Warren; and Doc Holliday, died out over the ensuing years. After the huge water pump at the Tombstone silver mines failed and the price of silver plummeted in the late 1880s, Tombstone had withered and died, and the exploits of the Earps and Doc Holliday were almost forgotten completely.

Old Tombstone Today

By the 1890s, most of the miners had left Cochise County (which included Tombstone). Since Tombstone was located in the middle of the desert, most people just boarded up their homes or stores and left town on horseback or in buggies and covered wagons. Most of them never returned, and simply abandoned in Tombstone whatever possessions they had been unable to take along with them.

As a result, the town – despite two major fires – remained much as it had been in Doc Holliday's and Wyatt Earp's days. There really wasn't any way to steal or even freely take large amounts of the relics left in the

Mary Katherine "Big Nose Kate" Harony, Doc's consort during his days in the West, was photographed here circa 1869. Though maligned in her later years, she was not unattractive as an adolescent. (Boyer Collection, Sharlot Hall Museum Archives)

town. Who would chance it across the desert? It remained this way for well over half a century, until the 1950s when American servicemen at nearby Fort Huachuca began taking weekend excursions to the historic site. It was also about this same time that several writers realized the value in publishing the biographies of the old West icons from this town.

Luckily, the handful of local townspeople who remained in Tombstone – which had become a virtual ghost town by the 1950s – apparently realized they had a money-maker on their hands. They banded together and created a historic district out of the town, preserving it for future generations.

Another view of the Dodge House, looking west down Front Street in Dodge City, Kansas. This photo was taken in 1874, just four years prior to the arrival of Doc in this cowtown. (Courtesy of Kansas State Historical Society, Topeka)

A few years after arriving out West, John Henry Holliday had this full-length photograph taken in 1879 when he lived in Prescott, Arizona. At the time, he was rooming with the acting governor of Arizona, John J. Gosper. (Photo courtesy of Craig Fouts)

Many of the same structures which the Earps, Doc Holliday, Buckskin Frank Leslie, William Barclay "Bat" Masterson, Ike Clanton, Johnny Ringo, Texas John Slaughter, the McLaury brothers, Turkey Creek Jack Johnson, Texas Jack Vermillion and many other figures of the old West had frequented, amazingly still stand today in Tombstone.

Though it burned in one of the town's two major fires, portions of the original O.K. Corral site still exist, as do the Wells-Fargo building; the billiard parlor (though re-built) in which Morgan Earp was mur-

Las Vegas, New Mexico, was well-known as a haven for individuals with tuberculosis in the late 19th century. The town's main attraction was its hot springs located several miles northwest of the town plaza. In 1878, Doc and Kate traveled to this town as "Dr. and Mrs. John H. Holliday." In 1879, Doc built and opened a 17-foot by 30-foot one-story saloon here (hardly visible, but located just beyond the second telegraph pole on the left). This view looks west along Centre Street, and was taken circa 1881. (Courtesy of Museum of New Mexico)

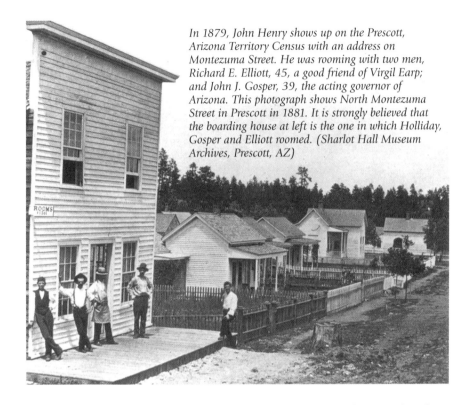

In 1879, John Henry shows up on the Prescott, Arizona Territory Census with an address on Montezuma Street. He was rooming with two men, Richard E. Elliott, 45, a good friend of Virgil Earp; and John J. Gosper, 39, the acting governor of Arizona. This photograph shows North Montezuma Street in Prescott in 1881. It is strongly believed that the boarding house at left is the one in which Holliday, Gosper and Elliott roomed. (Sharlot Hall Museum Archives, Prescott, AZ)

dered; the original Birdcage Theatre and the original Crystal Palace Saloon in which Holliday, the Earps and all the rest spent many days gambling and carousing. Even the home once owned and inhabited by Wyatt Earp on First Street still stands (as of this writing), as does the bank, and numerous other structures.

The Birdcage Theatre is one of the more prominent relics from that day. Built in December of 1881, it was a popular place to enjoy bawdy women, gambling and other forms of adult entertainment in old Tombstone. It has been preserved almost exactly as it existed in the 1880s – a museum to the town's famed former inhabitants.

A Life In The West

Holliday was 21 in 1872, when he began his travels. Interestingly, though his doctors had told him he had less than one year left on earth, he, in fact, lived for 15 more years, and in the interim, he traveled throughout the last frontier in the United States, earning a well-deserved reputation as one of the deadliest gunmen to grace the dusty streets of the old West.

Film sets from many of the old movies still exist at Old Tucson Studios. Judy Jackson takes a much-needed rest on the set from "Gunfight At The O.K. Corral," filmed in 1957 and starring Kirk Douglas (as Doc Holliday) and Burt Lancaster (as Wyatt Earp). The Tucson Depot - located just a couple of miles from this site was the location at which the real Earp and Holliday killed Frank Stillwell (who was one of the murderers of Morgan Earp) in 1882. (Photo by Olin Jackson)

Doc was also accused in print and folklore of being testy and irritable, but in retrospect, who wouldn't have been short-tempered under his circumstances. He was also known to be very gracious to those who were courteous to him, and his honor was the most valuable possession he owned. When bullied or persecuted as a result of his frail condition, John Henry Holliday invariably proved to be up to the challenge.

Though he often used what was known as a "pocket holster" (actually a reinforced pocket in his coat for carrying a weapon), he was one of the first gunmen to use a shoulder holster, and it has been documented in testimony from both Wyatt Earp and Bat Masterson that he was one of the deadliest gunmen they both had ever known.

Equally amazing, is the fact that Doc Holliday – despite the numerous gunfights in which he was involved – was not killed as a result of one of these conflicts. He was seriously wounded at least twice, and at the O.K. Corral gunfight, a glancing bullet grazed the pocket holster (in his coat) on his hip, giving him a bad

Though the streets are paved today and new buildings have filled in spots where older buildings had succumbed to neglect or one of the town's two major fires over the years, Allen (Main) Street in Tombstone is little-changed from the days of Doc Holliday and Wyatt Earp. A number of the original structures still stand. (Photo by Olin Jackson)

Wyatt Berry Stapp Earp was born in 1848 and died in 1929. Doc Holliday saved Wyatt's life on at least one, and possibly two occasions. As a result, Wyatt and Doc became life-long friends. They last saw each other in Denver, Colorado, in 1886, shortly before Doc's death in 1887.

bruise and a limp for several days, but he ultimately recovered in each instance. Few other prominent gunmen of the old West – Earp and Masterson interestingly being two of the few exceptions – endured this life without being killed. Earp, amazingly, was never even wounded.

All four of Wyatt's brothers were seriously wounded at some point in their lives, and two of them were killed. His brother Morgan was assassinated in Tombstone in 1882, and Warren was killed in a bar fight in Wilcox, Arizona, just a few miles away several years later. James Butler "Wild Bill" Hickok was killed in Deadwood, South Dakota. Johnny Ringo and most of the Clantons and McLaurys were killed in and around Tombstone in the 1880s. William "Billy the Kid" Bonney was killed in New Mexico in 1881. Jesse James, Pat Garrett, Butch Cassidy and the Sundance Kid, Billy Claiborne and many others all also met with bloody deaths. Doc and Wyatt, however, seemed almost invulnerable to bullets, despite their lifestyles.

A Friendship With Earp

Doc and Wyatt had become fast

Morgan Earp, younger brother of Wyatt, was born in 1851, the same year as Doc. The two men became fast friends in Tombstone, drinking and carousing, and protecting each other. Doc was particularly bereaved when Morgan was murdered in Campbell & Hatch Saloon in Tombstone in 1882, and sought vengeance - with Wyatt - on the younger Earp's killers. (Glenn G. Boyer Collection)

The Bird Cage Theatre is one of the original structures still standing from the days of the Old West in Tombstone. Though it was not built until December of 1881, the Bird Cage almost certainly was patronized by Doc. This structure is also the site at which Wyatt Earp reportedly met Josephine Sarah Markus, his future wife, who was a member of one of the theatrical productions that regularly came to town. After being boarded up for perhaps 40 years, this structure was reopened as a tourist attraction, and still contains many of its original furnishings. (Photo by Olin Jackson)

friends in Dodge City, Kansas, while Wyatt was a deputy city marshal there. Doc reportedly came to Wyatt's rescue (possibly saving his life) on two separate occasions – once in Dodge, and once again later in Tombstone – and Wyatt never forgot it. Though they quarreled in 1882 and went their separate ways, the two men remained close friends nevertheless to the end.

Wyatt was quoted as saying he enjoyed Doc's company because the clever dentist made him laugh. Doc was indeed known to have quite a sense of humor, as well as a love of practical jokes. According to one documented account, on one occasion when a stranger rode into Tombstone wearing a fancy suit and derby hat, Doc followed him throughout the

This corner site (left) was once the Oriental Saloon in which Wyatt Earp owned and operated a gambling concession, and in which Doc Holliday gambled and became embroiled in several gunfights in 1881. The Oriental was also the site of a vicious brawl between Doc and saloon owner Milt Joyce in which Doc - always willing to fight - was beaten unconscious. In the street (left foreground), Tombstone Marshal Virgil Earp was shot and crippled for life on the evening of December 28, 1881, as he walked from the Oriental on his way to the Crystal Palace Saloon on the opposite side of the street. (Photo by Olin Jackson)

35

One of John Henry Holliday's former haunts – the Eagle Brewery/Crystal Palace Saloon – as it looks today. (Photo by Olin Jackson)

town, gleefully ringing a hand-held dinner bell everywhere the man went – much to the well-dressed gentleman's uncomfortable chagrin.

There is so much history in the little town of Tombstone, that one would be well-advised to spend at least a weekend in explorations there if ever a visit is made to this historic site. Above and beyond the commercial buildings and homes in the town associated with Holliday and the Earps, many other sites in that vicinity were often frequented by other individuals who later gained fame on the frontier.

Ultimately, in their last days in the Tombstone area in 1882, Doc, Wyatt Earp, Warren Earp, Texas Jack Vermillion and a handful of other close friends began what was known as "the Vendetta Ride." They hunt-

This view of Allen Street (looking westward) in Tombstone was photographed in 1880. Despite being a silver strike boomtown, it is easy to see how the heat of the sun kept the town's inhabitants off the streets during the day. This view, at the intersection of 5th and Allen streets, shows the Eagle Brewery building (right) with the Crystal Palace Saloon occupying the lower level of the building. This saloon was a favorite of Holliday's, and he spent many hours here drinking and gambling.

The interior of the Crystal Palace Saloon was photographed in the 1880s. It was at these tables that John Henry "Doc" Holliday spent much of his time gambling. This photograph, no doubt, was taken by the town's venerable photographer, Camillus S. Fly, in whose rooming house Doc Holliday took up quarters during his stay in Tombstone.

ed down the outlaws who had assassinated one Earp (Morgan) and maimed another (Virgil) for life and who had been protected for years by a corrupt judicial system in Cochise County. Months later, when much of the outlaw element had been "eliminated" (by what some described as vigilante justice), Doc, Wyatt and Warren left forever, wandering anew in the West, searching once again for more adventure.

For the rest of their days, both Doc and Wyatt did nothing more than travel and enjoy life. Neither of them ever owned a home of any substance after leaving Tombstone (Doc never owned a home at all, preferring to live in hotels and rooming houses his entire adult life), and they both literally went wherever the wind blew them.

After the Vendetta Ride, Doc, Wyatt, Warren, Texas Jack Vermillion, Turkey Creek Jack Johnson and Dan Tipton drifted east to New Mexico Territory. Eventually, Doc, Wyatt, Warren and Tipton drifted northward up to Colorado, to the gold and silver mining towns which offered a refuge from the Cochise County, Arizona authorities, and an opportunity for gambling which both men needed to generate income. The Earps and Tipton spent the summer of 1882 in Gunnison, with Doc visiting them there for a brief time.

Approximately four years later in 1886 - just a short time before he died - Doc met Wyatt one last time. It was in Denver, Colorado. Doc was extremely ill by that point, and they both knew he couldn't last much longer. According to the memoirs of Josephine Sara Marcus (Wyatt's common-law wife), Wyatt told Doc, "Isn't it strange that if not for you I wouldn't be alive today, yet, you must go first."

Josephine said that as Wyatt and Doc parted that day, Doc threw his arm over Wyatt's shoulder saying "Good-bye old friend. It'll be a long time before we meet again." Josephine said that at those words, the great Wyatt Earp wept as he watched his old friend walk quickly away in an unstable gait.

The now-famous shooting which occurred near the O.K. Corral in Tombstone, Arizona Territory on October 26, 1881 is very realistically portrayed in this illustration by Mark Warren. All the participants appear very nearly in the spots at which they stood when the shooting occurred. This incident, more than any other, galvanized public attention upon not only the Earp brothers, but John Henry "Doc" Holliday as well, earning them lasting fame in the annals of American history. Holliday appears in the street (center) holding the shotgun. (Illustration by Mark Warren)

Mannequins representing the participants in the gunfight near the O.K. Corral have been positioned today in the approximate spot upon which the individuals stood on October 26, 1881. John Henry Holliday is represented by the dark figure (right rear) with the shotgun near the entryway. (Photo by Olin Jackson)

ABOVE LEFT: Frank McLaury was photographed sometime prior to the gunfight near the O.K. Corral in Tombstone. Doc Holliday delivered one of the three fatal shots that killed McLaury in the famous October 26, 1881 shoot-out. ABOVE RIGHT: It is a documented fact that Doc delivered the gunshot that sent Tom McLaury to the hereafter. Tom and his brother Frank were never convicted of any crimes, and are believed to have been reasonably decent men for cattle thieves.

The victims of the 1881 gunfight near the O.K. Corral were buried in Boot Hill just outside Tombstone. Frank McLaury, Tom McLaury and Billy Clanton all went to the hereafter after a quick but fierce 30-second shoot-out. (Photo by Olin Jackson)

This photograph, one of the most famous taken in the Old West, is believed to have been captured by Camillus S. Fly, venerable photographer for many years in Tombstone, Arizona Territory. Pictured here are the victims of the shoot-out near the O.K. Corral in Tombstone: Frank McLaury, Billy Clanton, and Tom McLaury. Two of these fatalities were attributed to Doc Holliday.

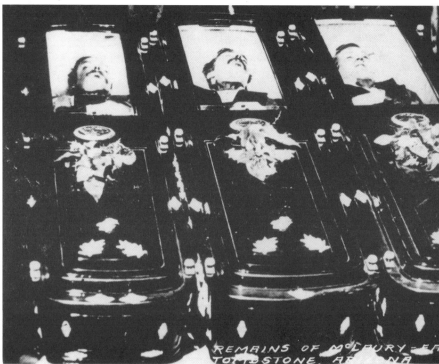

Confrontations In Colorado

As his infirmities gained the upper hand in the mid-1880s, more and more individuals sought a reputation as the person who finally bested the famous Doc Holliday.

It was the wildlife and gold in the Rocky Mountains of the West which attracted the early miners and trappers as the last frontier in America was being settled in the 19th century. And with the gold-mining towns came intrepid adventurers and gamblers like John Henry Holliday.

Despite the many things that are known about him, Holliday is, in many ways, an enigma – a mysterious individual. He traveled aimlessly throughout the West in the dying days of the frontier. He left few writings of his experiences, so there are many gaps in his collective history. Newspaper accounts of that time were notoriously inaccurate and sometimes vir-

John Henry Holliday as he appeared in the later years of his life. Gone was the vitality of youth even though he was only in his thirties, age-wise. (Photo courtesy of the Colorado Historical Society)

tually fictitious, and many of the letters he sent back home to family and friends were later destroyed or lost.

It is known, however, that once out West, Doc had no intention of returning to his Georgia home. Whether this was due to his gambling and widely-reported gunfights, or to his debilitating health, is unknown today.

Despite their beauty, the Rockies in Colorado must have been very taxing for Doc toward the latter portion of the 1880s. His tortured lungs had been seriously impaired by the tuberculosis bacterium eating away within him. He must have been constantly out of breath, often wondering if he was going to make it to the next day.

By this point, however, the die had been cast. He had little left to live for, and no way to make a living except the gambling trade. His terrible coughing fits had eliminated any possibility of the pursuit of the dental profession for which he had been trained. He spent a substantial amount of time in Denver from 1882-1884. His last days, however, were spent in the mining towns of Leadville and Glenwood Springs, Colorado.

From Arizona To Colorado
Approximately six months after the shoot-out at the O.K. Corral, Doc, Wyatt and Warren Earp, Turkey Creek Jack Johnson, Texas Jack Vermillion, Dan Tipton, and perhaps one or two others involved in what became known as "the Vendetta Ride" in Arizona, had left that state for New Mexico. They had traveled together for a period of time, but had eventually decided to split up, with Doc and Dan Tipton traveling on to Denver. Wyatt – and presumably brother Warren – headed to the seclusion and safety of Gunnison, Colorado, where they were joined for a short time by Doc for a friendly reunion during the summer of 1882.

On the way to Denver earlier that year, Doc reportedly had met up with several other old acquaintances in Pueblo: Bat Masterson, Sam Osgood and an individual known only as Texas George. The men reportedly planned to attend the horse races in Denver and checked into the Windsor Hotel on the northeast corner of Eighteenth and Larimer streets.

The five-floor Windsor was a 300-room hotel – one of Denver's finest – and with its white marble floors, plush red carpeting and sixty-foot mahogany bar, it was just the type lavish establishment that the gambler from Georgia enjoyed.

Unfortunately, Doc's penchant for trouble caught up with him here once again. An individual named Perry Mallen arrested Holliday on an old fraudulent murder charge from Doc's days in Arizona Territory. Mallen identified himself as an associate and envoy of Sheriff Johnny Behan of Cochise County in Arizona, where Doc was also "Wanted" for his participation in the Vendetta Ride.

As a result, Doc was temporarily jailed in Colorado, but ultimately was rescued several weeks later by Bat Masterson, who, as a law enforcement official himself, indicated he was taking Doc into his custody for the return to Arizona, then merely escorted him out of town and set him free. Though Masterson personally considered Holliday distasteful, he came to the tubercular gambler's assistance as a special favor to his friend Wyatt Earp, who had come to his (Bat's) aid on more than one occasion in the past.

Of all the towns in the West, Doc preferred Denver. Its comfortable and modern hotels, gambling establishments and opportunities for entertainment suited his nature. He traveled back and forth to Denver while living in nearby Leadville, and while on the run from corrupt Arizona authorities in 1882 who sought him for his involvement in the Vendetta Ride with the Earp faction. When in Denver, Doc frequented the Palace Theatre, as did Wyatt Earp and Bat Masterson. Masterson even managed it for a time.

Denver To Leadville

In a further attempt to escape his past, and to continue his livelihood in gambling, Doc left Denver and traveled by stage approximately 125 miles southwestward to the town of Leadville. This community had been a mining boomtown since 1877 when a rich outcropping of silver ore had been discovered. By the time Doc arrived in July of 1882, mining of the precious metal had slowed, but there were still many gambling opportunities at the scores of saloons and bordellos in this boomtown.

One can only guess today at Holliday's perception of Leadville back in the 1880s. Did he enjoy the snow, or did he simply find it to be another impediment to life? What was it like in the bleak shadows of the Rockies in a time when there was no indoor plumbing in most establishments, and no warm comfortable automobiles in which to travel about? Granted there were trains, and Doc reportedly made use of them whenever possible, but more often than not, he either traveled on horseback or within the shivering confines of a jarring stagecoach, and in 1882, there was no train to Leadville.

When he arrived in the high mountain town, Doc found employment as a faro dealer at Cyrus "Cy" Allen's Monarch Saloon which was located at

320 Harrison Avenue. However, he didn't last long there. He no doubt was heavily dependent upon alcohol by this time, and it quite possibly affected his ability to perform his job. One must remember that by this time, Doc's best years were behind him. Whatever the circumstances, Doc's employment at Allen's Saloon ended almost as quickly as it had begun.

According to reports, Holliday found new work nearby as a faro dealer in one of the clubrooms of Hyman's Saloon owned by Mannie Hyman. It was located at 316 Harrison Avenue next door to the Tabor Opera House. Both of these structures, surprisingly, still stand as of this writing in downtown Leadville. Doc apparently decided this was a good spot to put down some roots. He was able to obtain a room upstairs on the northwest corner of this building. Today, this room is maintained as a memorial to the famous gambler.

Bleak Existence

Doc's tiny room – seven by fourteen feet – was his refuge in these final years. It gave him a beautiful – albeit bleak no doubt to him – view of the snow-covered Rockies. When he wasn't sleeping, Doc almost always could be found in Hyman's saloon, dealing the faro games, or, across the street at John G. Morgan's Board of Trade Saloon where he often sat on the player's side of the table, playing stud poker. The Board of Trade also still stands as of this writing.

According to reports, during the years 1882 to 1886, Doc occasionally visited most of the gambling houses along Harrison Street, plying his trade. However, by this time, his physical condition had debilitated his skills as a gambler, and his winnings had declined considerably. He was often short of money.

It seems almost pitiful to imagine Doc Holliday by this point in his life. He was very quickly succumbing to the tuberculosis ravaging his lungs and his health in general. He had always been slight in stature, but had been lightning quick with strong hands and arms, and usually capable of handling himself when confronted. His growing alcoholism, however, had affected his diet – and thus his weight and strength. He had also lost most of his stamina due to the tuberculosis in his lungs and to two bouts of pneumonia with which he suffered during this period. In short, Doc Holliday was a pitiful sight in the mid-1880s.

When the whiskey – with which Doc was liberally self-medicating himself – ceased to calm the growing pain and on-going destruction in his lungs, the once handsome dentist and gambler reportedly found another medication – laudanum. A local druggist who owned an apothecary at the corner of Sixth and Harrison streets, befriended Holliday and reportedly provided the drug to him.

His growing dependency on laudanum coupled with the severe bouts of pneumonia weakened Holliday even more. He was able to sustain himself with an occasional win at the card tables, but it was a meager existence at best.

Becoming A Target

As a result of his obviously weak physical state, the wolves began circling. Doc increasingly became a target for roughneck gamblers and predators in general who sought to earn a name for themselves by becoming the person who out-gunned or defeated the great Doc Holliday.

In his prime, Doc had usually needed only to identify himself to most belligerents – even vicious ones – in order to avoid a fight. However, by the time he reached Leadville, he

William J. "Billy" Allen was photographed circa 1895, in Carrollton, Missouri, approximately 11 years after being wounded by Holliday in Leadville. In this photo even the least discriminating eye can see Allen looked every bit the part of the bullying predator described in historic accounts. He had assumed he would severely beat, if not kill, the sick and weakened Holliday, but after experiencing the wrath of the Georgian's Colt's .41 revolver, Allen never again confronted Holliday.

was so obviously weak and debilitated that he had become an easy mark. More and more, the stronger bullies pushed ever harder to goad Holliday into a fist or gunfight.

Though he was weak and disabled, Doc – to his credit – was never a coward, and he would not be bullied, regardless of the circumstances. For this reason, Leadville, Colorado, enjoys the unique distinction of being the site of John Henry Holliday's last gunfight.

Two of Doc's old Tombstone, Arizona, enemies – William "Billy" Allen and Johnny Tyler – unfortunately were living in Leadville at the time of Doc's residence there. According to Karen Holliday Tanner in

Doc Holliday: A Family Portrait, (University of Oklahoma Press) Allen was a former Leadville policeman who had been a friend of Ike Clanton – Doc's old Tombstone nemesis. Allen had even served as a prosecution witness during the O.K. Corral shooting inquest and had testified against Doc.

". . . he (Allen) had accompanied Reuben Coleman on the day of the gunfight in Tombstone," Ms. Tanner writes. *"They had walked down Allen Street through the O.K. Corral to the front of Camillus S. Fly's Gallery (behind Fly's Boarding House). It was believed by some, and certainly by Doc, that during the fracas, Allen had fired a number of shots aimed at both Holliday and the Earps from the passageway between Fly's buildings. After coming to Leadville, Allen had been a part-time policeman and had been hired as a bartender at the Monarch Saloon."*

During the winter of 1883-84, Doc found work at Mannie Hyman's Saloon at 316 Harrison, photographed here circa 1880s. It was here on the afternoon of August 19, 1884, that Doc confronted bully Billy Allen, wounding him severely with his Colt's 41 revolver as Allen stepped through the doorway of the saloon. This was the last gunfight in which Doc was involved. (Courtesy of Denver Public Library)

Confronting Johnny Tyler

Ms. Tanner also explains how Johnny Tyler – after the Tombstone years – was dealing faro at the Casino Gambling Hall in Leadville. During the Tombstone years in the early 1880s, Tyler had been forcibly removed from the Oriental Saloon by Wyatt Earp in order to rid the establishment of a troublemaker and to give Wyatt the opportunity to open a gambling concession there himself. Doc had been present at this altercation and had berated Tyler as he was being ejected, and Tyler had never forgotten it, carrying the memory of this humiliation with him for years thereafter.

In 1884, after Doc had departed Arizona Territory for Colorado, Tyler chanced upon the by-then weak and

Photographed in 2002, this view shows the lower level of the building which once housed Mannie Hyman's Saloon in which Doc Holliday was a faro dealer off and on from 1883 to 1887. It was also just inside the front door of this building that Holliday, in his last gunfight in 1884, wounded and almost killed the bullying Billy Allen. Holliday also roomed in this building on the second floor. The window of his room is visible (above, left) at the corner. (Photo by Olin Jackson)

vulnerable gambler in Leadville, and he couldn't believe his luck. Along with Billy Allen who also resided in Leadville at this time, he (Tyler) immediately began plotting his revenge against Holliday.

Doc's luck couldn't have been much worse at this time. Not only had his gambling skills been sorely diminished which had reduced him virtually to a beggar's status, he had also been forced into the unenviable position of having to request a five dollar loan from none other than the vengeful Allen. It was this indebtedness which set the stage for the final drama in Doc's life.

"Allen, knowing of Doc's dire straits (financially), had willingly loaned the money, assuming that Doc would have difficulty repaying the debt," Mrs. Tanner writes. *"This would give Allen justification to goad the weak, sick Holliday into a gunfight. Doc had borrowed the money with the promise to repay it in less than a week. Seven days later, he had to go to Billy and humbly explain that he had not been able to collect an outstanding debt and therefore did not have the money (to repay Allen)."*

For a number of weeks in Leadville, Doc was continuously insulted and humiliated by Johnny Tyler and his cohorts. In an earlier day, they would not have dared to confront and challenge him in such a manner, but in 1884, Doc was only a shadow of his former persona, and his antagonizers knew it. They relentlessly taunted him, threatening him with gunplay, but by this time, Doc no longer even carried a gun. He was virtually destitute, and could not afford to pay a fine for possession of a

FINAL GUNFIGHT - Billy Allen had been a friend of the Clantons, a gang of outlaws which had opposed Doc Holliday and the Earps during the gunfight at O.K. Corral in Tombstone, Arizona in 1881. Allen had also testified against Holliday in the inquest held after that gunfight. For this reason, he was a long-time enemy. This view shows the front portion of what was the interior of Hyman's Saloon in 1884. At that time, a bar existed along the wall to the right, and Holliday was positioned just behind it near the front window. After threatening Holliday, Allen entered the doorway which at that time existed where the gift items framed in the big picture window (left center) exist today. Holliday grabbed his Colt's .41 revolver from behind the bar and fired as Allen entered, seriously wounding him. (Photo by Olin Jackson)

firearm in the city limits. After having been stopped and searched a number of times by the Leadville police, he was very careful not to violate the city ordinance by carrying a gun anymore.

"Words passed between him and Tyler and his cronies at Hyman's Bar, and several of them called him to 'pull his gun,'" a local Leadville newspaper reporter wrote at the time. "He said he had none, and as he passed outside, he was called filthy names. . . Next day, he told this writer, with tears of rage coming to his eyes as he talked, that they were insulting and humiliating him because they knew he could not retaliate."

Allen Eats Lead

Billy Allen, who had been waiting for his opportunity, finally issued Doc an ultimatum: Pay the debt by noon of the following Tuesday or face the threat of severe violence.

"When Tuesday arrived, some of Doc's friends went to his room and told him that Allen was looking for him with a gun," Ms. Tanner continued.

Owned as of this writing by Ms. Mary McVicar, the old Hyman Saloon building at 316 Harrison Avenue offers only gift items today instead of gambling and liquor. On the walls above – well out of the reach of patrons – Ms. McVicar has displayed a collection of firearms which date to the 1880s, including one which she maintains was owned by Holliday. The pressed tin ceiling (top) is original to the building. (Photo by Olin Jackson)

". . . On the stairway down into the saloon, Doc asked Mannie Hyman to get an officer for protection. He continued into the saloon but did not find Allen. He asked his friend and fellow boarder Frank Lomeister, who was working the day shift as bartender, to get Capt. Edmond Bradbury of the Leadville Police Department or Marshal Harvey Faucett, adding that he did not want to sit around for the afternoon unprotected."

Doc was much more cautious by this point in his life. According to reports of this famous incident, he returned to his room where he remained in the tiny enclosure until approximately five o'clock in the afternoon. He knew however, that he eventually would have to go back down to the saloon to work, but he also knew he couldn't afford the fine if he was caught with a weapon. He therefore instructed one of his friends to take his (Doc's) Colt's .41 revolver down and hide it behind the bar. He then went down to the saloon himself and sat near the end of the bar behind the cigar case where he could quickly grab his gun if necessary.

It was obviously a very dramatic setting, one more characteristic of Doc's earlier days in Dodge City or Tombstone. According to reports of the incident, Billy Allen eventually did enter the saloon, and he had the misfortune to have his hand in his pocket as if holding a weapon.

When Doc saw Allen's hand in his gun pocket, that was all the threat he needed. Without hesitation, Doc – in a flashback to his old glory days – immediately grabbed his pistol and fired a round at Allen. The bullet struck the unfortunate victim in the fleshy part of his upper arm and severed an artery. When Allen fell to the floor, Doc fired at him yet again. He meant to end this threat once and for all. This round struck the door sill, barely missing Allen's head. Before he could get off another shot, Doc was grabbed by Henry Killerman who wrestled the gun away. This action almost certainly saved the life of one Billy Allen.

Doc was arrested and charged with "Assault with intent to commit murder." He was locked up in the jail and his bail was set at five thousand dollars. In an earlier day, John Henry Holliday could have easily raised that amount to bail himself out of jail, but by the time of his days in Leadville, Doc was living virtually hand-to-mouth. For that reason, $5,000 was an impossibly high bail for him to raise, and he must surely have thought he was going to be incarcerated in the cold damp jail for months until his trial date arrived.

Photographed sometime after 1898 during one of the Strawberry Days parades in Glenwood Springs, this funeral coach from 1885 possibly transported Holliday's body to the vicinity of Linwood Cemetery on November 8, 1887. (Courtesy of Frontier Historical Society)

Mary Katherine Harony Cummings ("Big-Nosed Kate") was photographed here circa 1890. Gone was the limited beauty she had enjoyed as a young adult. (A.W. Bork and Glenn G. Boyer Collection)

On Trial For Assault

Interestingly, though it has seldom been publicized, Doc had a number of good friends in his later years. Two of these stepped forward immediately. John G. Morgan and Samuel Houston, co-owners of the Board of Trade Saloon, arrived the next morning and immediately posted bail for Doc.

In the trial that followed, a number of eye-witnesses testified to the threats that had been issued at Doc by Allen, and the circumstances of the shooting that had followed. Doc took the stand on his own behalf and explained the details of the loan and the subsequent threats.

"I saw Allen coming in with his hand in his pocket, and I thought my life was as good to me as his was to him," Holliday explained in his courtroom testimony. *"I fired the shot and he fell on the floor, and (I) fired the second shot; I knew that I would be a child in his hands if he got hold of me; I weigh 122 pounds; I think Allen weighs 170; I have had pneumonia three or four times. I don't think I would have been able to protect myself against him."*

The jury ultimately returned a verdict of "Not Guilty" in the case of *People vs John Henry Holliday*. Following this last gunfight, the curtain essentially came down on the life of Doc Holliday, and it ended completely his gunfighting days. He was never again involved in a shooting incident.

Not too long after the trial, Doc must have felt the urge to move on to another town. He first took a short trip back to Denver one last time before returning briefly to Leadville.

In the interim, Doc had heard of the steamy sulphur waters at Glenwood Springs in northwestern Colorado, and of the fact that some individuals had gone there for the treatment of various health problems. This town, no doubt, was doubly attractive, since it was known as a health resort, and it also was a mining town too, with many saloons and other gaming establishments which offered Doc yet another opportunity to ply the gambling trade. It offered just the opportunity Doc sought at this point in his life. Once again, he found himself on an uncomfortable trip in a jarring stagecoach in the cold Colorado Rockies.

Last Days In Glenwood

Today, Glenwood Springs isn't much larger than it was in Doc's day in 1887. (It might even be smaller.) The warm springs are still active and frequented by many individuals interested in the curative qualities of the waters.

Doc had traveled by stagecoach from Leadville to Glenwood Springs in May of 1887. He reportedly had traveled to the town in particular to breathe the sulphur vapors in a mistaken assumption that they would help his sick lungs. Ironically, rather than curing Doc's ills, the acidic and acrid vapors caused him to cough even worse, hastening his demise.

When he reached town, his appearance reportedly was that of an individual well-advanced in years, with silver hair and an emaciated stooped posture. According to a news article of that day, "He walked down the street with a feeble tread and a downcast look. If he heard a [gun]shot, he raised his head with eager attention and glanced this way and that." Even in 1887, Glenwood Springs obviously was still somewhat wild and unsettled.

Doc reportedly was admired by many residents in Glenwood Springs in the weeks immediately following his arrival, and in the few months that he was there, he cultivated numerous friends. For a number of weeks, he reportedly attempted once again to ply his old trade at the gambling tables. By this point, however, he simply was no longer able to participate. Gone was the vitality which had served him so well in Kansas and Arizona. With the departure of his strength and stamina also went his will to live. He no doubt knew his last days were really upon him at this point.

His spirits understandably were low, and, according to Karen Holliday Tanner, Doc had written to his former consort – Mary Katherine "Kate" Harony in Globe, Arizona – telling her he was traveling to Glenwood Springs, and asking her to join him there. By this point, Doc must have known he was fast approaching the time when he would need someone to physically assist him with the rudimentary tasks of daily life. He no doubt knew of no one to call upon except Kate.

Doc and Kate had traveled many miles together earlier in their lives. They had enjoyed many adventures across the West in places like Las Vegas, New Mexico; Dodge City, Kansas; Tucson and Tombstone, Arizona. This bond no doubt held them together as Doc fought for life in the final months of his life.

In Kate's Care

Many accounts today indicate Doc died alone and abandoned in the Hotel Glenwood in his last days. One recently-discovered (2004) and very credible documented record – explained in detail in the following chapter – however, indicates an entirely different scenario.

Whatever the circumstances, Doc took a room at the Hotel Glenwood on the northeast corner of Grand Avenue and Eighth Street in Glenwood Springs. This exceptional hotel had just recently been built (1886), and was among the finest in the West at that time. It offered among its amenities electric lights and both hot and cold running water in every room. The water was pumped directly from the Grand (later renamed Colorado) River, since there was no water system in the town, with the sewage returned directly into the river.

Most of the old saloons and gambling establishments in Glenwood Springs are gone today, replaced by more modern structures. Tragically, the Hotel Glenwood burned to the ground on December 14, 1945, killing five people, and destroying forever the last home ever known by John Henry Holliday.

Though the town fathers of Glenwood Springs seem to have paid limited heed toward historic preservation over the years, the community yet retains a somewhat scenic air, unique with its warm springs. The stark Rockies are still startlingly beautiful, but they must have been cold and forbidding to Doc in his dying days.

During the last 57 days of his life, John Henry Holliday reportedly rose from his bed at the Hotel Glenwood only twice. He and Kate reportedly relied upon the bellhop to serve them their meals so that Kate did not have to leave his bedside.

It is poignant to imagine Kate attending to him in these last days. She easily could have ignored his request to join him in Colorado. She must have known the task of caring for him would not be pleasant. She reportedly never wavered from her duties however, and even used her meager savings to support them after Doc could no longer work. In her later years, she said she considered her relationship with Doc to be a marriage.

All the years of smoking, drinking, poor diet and poor care finally caught up with the famed gambler. Pneumonia and tuberculosis ultimately combined to do what many gunmen over the years had failed to accomplish. By the third week in October of 1887, Doc was delirious, and by Monday of November 7, he reportedly was unable to speak, so many researchers and writers maintain it is unlikely he ever uttered the now-famous last words, "This is funny," as claimed in folklore. He died on November 8, 1887.

Alexander Harony, brother to Kate ("Big Nose") Harony, lived with his family at Penny Hot Springs in the Crystal Valley near Glenwood Springs, Colorado. It was to this cabin that Kate reportedly brought Doc Holliday for recuperation prior to a return to Glenwood Springs shortly before his death. (Glenn G. Boyer Collection)

Myths Of The Man

Also contrary to popular myth and modern movie portrayals, Doc Holliday did not die in the Glenwood Springs Sanitarium. There was no sanitarium in Glenwood Springs in 1887. Doc Holliday died in his room in the Hotel Glenwood.

Mystery seems to follow Doc right into the grave. The actual site of his burial is not known today. There is a Doc Holliday gravesite in Linwood Cemetery in Glenwood Springs, but it is an acknowledged fact that most historians believe Doc Holliday very likely is not buried there. Even the cemetery records state only that it is believed that he is "buried somewhere in this cemetery."

On the day of Doc's funeral, the weather reportedly was bitterly cold. Along with John Henry, one other recently-deceased gentleman was to be buried in Linwood Cemetery on the same day. On the day of the burial, the trail up to the cemetery was impassable, and, as a result, Doc and the other deceased individual were buried by the side of the road somewhere along the route up to the cemetery, the intention being that they would be exhumed in the spring and re-buried in the cemetery.

The following spring, however, things changed a bit. The individual buried beside Doc apparently had family in the Glenwood Springs area who readily paid to have their loved one dug up and re-buried in Linwood. Doc, however, had no family in the area, and according to reports, no one was forthcoming to pay the fee to have him exhumed and re-buried. He, therefore, was left buried beside the road.

As time passed, local residents came and went and the grave of the famed John Henry Holliday surprisingly was forgotten. It was only in the mid- to late-20th century that local residents – realizing the historic and tourism-related value of Doc's burial site – began trying to re-locate his grave. Despite considerable efforts however, the gravesite remains a mystery. Today, the mortal remains of Dr. John Henry Holliday from Griffin and Valdosta, Georgia, quite possibly exist beneath someone's back porch or in someone's yard on the route up to Linwood Cemetery.

Other accounts differ with the above scenario. According to one, Doc's remains were indeed later dug up and re-buried in Linwood Cemetery, where they exist today. Another account maintains that they were dug up, but were transported – via the new railroad in Glenwood Springs – back to Georgia in the late 1880s, where they were re-buried in an unmarked grave in Griffin, Doc's birthplace.

Kate's Last Days

Interestingly, Doc's consort for all those years in Arizona and Colorado – Mary Katherine Horony – reportedly gathered up Doc's belongings from his room after his death, and shipped them to Doc's one true love – his cousin, Sister Mary Melanie of the Order of the Sisters of Mercy – who had entered a convent to become a nun after Doc left Atlanta, Georgia for the West.

After she had disposed of Doc's last possessions, Kate then left the sadness in Glenwood Springs forever, but reportedly remained for a time at her brother's home nearby in the Crystal Valley region of Colorado. On March 2, 1890, she married George M. Cummings in the mining town of Aspen, Colorado, a well-known ski resort today. The couple moved about the West before finally settling in Bisbee, Cochise County, Arizona, in 1895, just a few miles from Tombstone where Doc had gained so much fame in 1881-1882.

This marriage lasted approximately nine years before Kate left Mr. Cummings who was an alcoholic. (Kate enjoyed little if any luck in her selection of men.) On June 2, 1900, she accepted employment as the housekeeper of John J. Howard of Dos Cabezas, Arizona. She remained in his employ until Howard's death in 1930. On June 13, 1931, Kate wrote to Arizona Governor George W. Hunt requesting permission to live in the state-supported Arizona Pioneers Home in Prescott.

Governor Hunt reportedly granted Kate's request. For the last nine years of her life, Mary Katherine Cummings (nee Horony)–also known by many as "Big-Nose Kate"–lived out her final days in the town where, in 1880, she and Doc had spent time together just prior to his Tombstone days. She died on November 2, 1940, and was buried at the Pioneer Cemetery in Prescott.

Today, one can only imagine how John Henry Holliday felt in his last days, separated from his family and friends back in Georgia, as well as his surrogate family–the Earps–who, by that time, were scattered from Arizona to California. Thankfully, he did have Kate in his last days. She no doubt brought him comfort in his final hours.

It, however, seems a pity the last remains of one of the most famous and fabled of all the individuals of the old West, lie in an unknown and unmarked grave today, mysterious and yet respected even in death. Ironically, that's probably just the way Doc would have wanted it. His lonely wandering soul is finally at peace.

The "Gambling Room" of the Pioneer Saloon in Leadville, Colorado, no doubt was patronized by Doc at least once in the last year or two of his life. (Western History Collection, Denver Public Library)

The Last Days According To The *Sulphur, Oklahoma Headlight*

Though the actual circumstances of Doc's last days on this earth have been debated for years, one credible recently-discovered newspaper article may describe the true events, debunking previously-held notions.

Some writers and researchers have maintained that Doc spent his last days alone in the Hotel Glenwood, slowly wasting away until death finally took him. Other researchers, supported by at least one recently-discovered document, however, maintain an entirely different set of circumstances existed. Until recent times, no detailed first-hand account of Doc's last days was known to exist.

According to Karen Holliday Tanner, Doc sent for Big Nose Kate when he realized his last days were upon him, and she subsequently joined him and cared for him until he died. A recently discovered newspaper article, published in the February 14, 1899 issue of the *Sulphur Headlight* of Sulphur, Oklahoma, supports that contention, and provides many additional enlightening details about his final days as well.

The information was detailed by an individual by the name of Origen C. "Harelip Charlie" Smith, who, fittingly, was an ally of the Earps and Holliday during the volatile days in Tombstone, Arizona Territory, in 1880-1882. Smith was a business associate of Bob Winders in Tombstone, and soon had allied himself with the Earps in support of law and order in the frontier town. His days in that town were well-documented, and are a matter of public record today.

By coincidence, Smith found himself traveling in the same stagecoach to Glenwood Springs, Colorado, in 1887, and living in the same hotel there as Doc. He was present during Doc's dying days and was intimately familiar with the individuals present and the events surrounding this now-famous event.

Later, after moving back to Tombstone, Arizona, Smith, realizing the importance of the knowledge he carried with him, began writing down his memoirs for posterity. He reportedly sought out another old friend – Lundsford Bryant Shockley – to collaborate with him on the memoirs.

In 1899, Shockley reportedly shared the portion of Smith's memoirs involving Glenwood Springs with the publisher of the *Sulphur, Oklahoma Headlight*, and on February 14 of that year, the *Headlight* published the very interesting details of Doc's last days in Glenwood Springs. It is re-published here in its entirety, exactly as written by Smith, with the exception of quotation marks and paragraph delineations for ease of reading. The initial part of the article published in the *Headlight* was written from the editor's perspective, with the remainder from Smith's perspective. This captivating document reads as follows:

"The story comes to the *Headlight* from colleague Lundsford Shockley, resident of the Chickasaw Nations, Ardmore, Indian Territory. It is known that Mr. Shockley came to town by wagon early in the evening and boarded at the Hotel Sulphur Springs in preparation to meet the *Headlight* staff.

"It is apparent that connections to Mr. [Origen Charles] Smith came from Shockley's days with John Roberts of the [John] Slaughter crew, driving those vast Texas herds up to the San Pedro Valley. Shockley comments: 'We were encamped up in the Sierra Vistas in '81. On the first time out, many of the boys wanted to go to Tombstone and experience the town's pleasures. Tombstone was a mining camp built from the dust much like the old pueblo, Tucson, which offered a cowboy anything imaginable.'

"According to Charlie Smith, it was also a community built on politics; 'a common cause of much of the troubles there.'

"When upon reading the Harelip Smith papers, I might comment that the significance surrounds the death of John H. Holliday, known as Doc, on November 8, 1887, where Smith occupied a room across the hallway from him in the Hotel Glenwood, some twelve years ago. It is important to note that Origen Smith's recollections serve as a standard account of the dentist's last days in Glenwood Springs who wrote on his Sol Israel stationery on October 8, 1887, that 'Holliday was confined to his bed by the local physician who had told his mistress: "I have done all that can be done. It is in John's hands now. And God's."'

"Origen Smith gives an account of Doc Holliday's arrival to the mountain resort on May 24, 1887 [as follows]:

"'The Concorde coach had slammed into the rocks along the narrow gauge of mountain road near Carbondale, which damaged the wheel at the rear of the coach which suddenly ended their journey until a mechanic could be brought in from several miles distant. The narrow gauge out of Leadville was hard on Holliday and its three passengers but it was the best means of travel for the day.

"'The three passengers on the stage knew who Doc Holliday was, but I doubt they had heard of Origen Smith when I arrived on the Leadville laundry train with a group of miners who flooded Leadville when Hoarse Tabot [Horace "Haw" Tabor] discovered the "Matchbox" [Matchless] mine. We were packed in that coach like a can of sardines, fighting to get out.

"'I had boarded the coach heeled but concealed it inside my coat just as Doc had done that day when all hell broke loose down at Montgomery's [the O.K. Corral]. In Tombstone, I had served as vigilance messenger for Colonel Wm. Herring, a prominent Tombstone attorney who's (sic) office located at 534 Freemont, served as a meeting place for many of Wyatt Earp's backers. In 1882, I had been a messenger for Wyatt Earp, joining his federal posse after the death of his brother by cowards.

"'Experience had taught me for a man like Holliday – who told me once that I should join the game – that he did not fear death. It was the living that he feared most. The fear of not going out game. Many times I had seen Doc cry tears from the agony the dreadful disease scourged him when the whiskey failed to do its work.

"'The trip from Leadville was hard on Doc. The jolting from the narrow gauge would cause him to cough up pieces of lung and blood. It was about two o'clock when the stage reached the Hotel Glenwood. Kate said it was May 24th.

"'Doc was coughing from almost each breath and upon arrival, had to use his cane to support his weight. He was very frail in body when I saw him, and his hair was a silver gray. His face showed the lines of age and he looked sick in the eyes. His appearance resembled that of an older man, since pulling out of Hooker's Ranch [where the Vendetta riders were temporarily protected in 1882].

"'One might argue that Doc was content in his actions and that his daily consumption of whiskey came to be his only escape from his suffering. I was rightly taken with the general surroundings of Glenwood Springs upon reaching Eighth Avenue, holding my duffle and looking for the hotel.

"'Kate had told me Doc was boarding. All I wanted was to register and find a bathhouse. I had run into Kate in the lobby who had sent this young bellhop, whom Doc had nicknamed Kenny [Art Kendrick], on an errand.

"'The welcome feeling I experienced far exceeded that of Tombstone I soon discovered. The district was full of excitement when the train pulled into the station house. I recall most of all how many people were about on the streets.

"'There was a definite resemblance to Denver; the big blue sky and the "Rockies," that seem to surround the town, which I would soon see was a perfect view from Doc's hotel window.

"'The Denver and Rio Grande was due to arrive the following day [October 5], and the town was full of anticipation of the arrival of the new iron horse. Banners swung across streets, and merchant signs from store front windows. Great expectations filled the streets.

"'I refrained from the moment and walked in the lobby of the Hotel Glenwood. The lobby was furnished with fine "Victorian" trimmings and elaborate knotted-Persian carpets, reminded me of the Cosmopolitan and Grand hotels in Tombstone, and the White Club House Room in Denver.

"'There was this need to put down words on paper since leaving Hooker's Ranch in '82, but it was Kate's enduring patience and devotion to Doc that gave me my inspiration to tell the story.

"'There was a sense of fatalism in Kate's voice, yet talk of the springs which had brought Doc to Glenwood was the last hope the West had to offer a lunger like Doc. I suppose if there was a chance for Doc's health to improve, he would take up its resources of Glenwood Springs.

"'Writing this down is not to judge him for past actions, but to understand him. Doc's memory seemed to be unaffected at times, although he lost much of his lungs over the years out West since leaving his beloved Georgia. I know the whiskey came to be his only escape from the pain that came with the consumption, and his desperate longing for home.

"'There is no doubt that the short time Doc lived inside the Hotel

Glenwood, [it] became his sanctuary. What transpired within the walls will leave a lasting impression. One that is etched in my memory.

"'Coming to Glenwood Springs with the miners in October, I found Doc delirious and dying. He had fallen to a pneumonia the local doctor said, and had not spoken a word in weeks. Kate was already there taken (sic) care of him when I arrived. She said Doc had sent word to her in Globe from Leadville and told her he was leaving after a bit of excitement with Will Allen, and was taking a stage to Glenwood Springs, in Garfield County to see if the sulphur springs would ease his consumption.

"'Kate's devotion to Doc was not surprising, for she remained by his side till the end. Doc had tolerated my presence in Tombstone, though suggested I join the game after Morg's death, since Morg and I had a fondness to billiards at Robert Hatch's. Doc was still a young man though he began to deteriorate in Denver and became more advanced as his struggle for pain was no longer at his control. Doc was at the point of never leaving his bed again.

"'I imagine Kate felt helpless not being able to ease his pain. Shortly after Doc arrived, he tryed (sic) dealing faro but no longer could keep up the long hours he was used to in Tombstone, for he tired easily. Walking from gambling house to gambling house became an exhausting event, and the treatments at the springs [never] seemed to have any effect.

"'Kate was their means for support, for Doc could not work. I would help to bring in money by doing odd jobs around town, and doing mechanic work for a blacksmith shop.

"'Since October, Doc hardly spoke and hardly sat up twice. Kate never wanted to be far from Doc. I consoled her and saw to it no harm came to Doc from the traffic coming and going inside the hotel. Doc had made many enemies in his life and perhaps [because of] the troubles Doc faced in Arizona and Colorado, she still sensed danger to him.

"'A light snow had fallen early in the morning and Kate had to shut the window in Doc's room. His breathing had become shallow overnight and the color in his face had turned pale. It is important to know the last day as I was in the hotel room with Doc and Kate as he clinged (sic) to life.

"'An era was ending Kate thought. I don't write about an era changing, but a man's life who was shaped around it. For Kate the day began to fall apart when I was told that Kate sent for the doctor and that I should return to Doc's room. It seemed strange for anyone beside Doc or Kate to summon me at once. I went, expecting the end had come.

"'In the lobby I had a strange feeling. Instead of the heavy traffic, there was this stillness in the hotel lobby as I hurried up to Doc's room. Then the bellhop told me that Doc was sitting up. I felt relief for Kate. For a moment I thought Doc had cheated death one last time.

"'Doc had been found that morning sitting up by the maid who had awoke (sic) Kate who had slept in Doc's chair that he liked sitting by the window in. The doctor was there when I got there. He was saying something to Kate, but his words didn't make her feel better.

"'For the first time in weeks, the details and the sound of Dr. B.'s [possibly Dr. Baldwin] voice was [sic] clear. She knew the end was upon him. Knowing Doc, I figured he might pull out another winning hand. It was not meant to be. This would be his last game.

"'I did not know the complete story from the doctor who had been making house calls to Doc's room the past few weeks. Though I never doubted his opinion. In the final hour I knew one thing. Doc was about to cash in his chips.

"'There were several Glenwood residents in the room, Sarah Copper [Sarah Field Cooper] and Walter Devereaux, whom (sic) shared a seat with Doc on the Concorde stage.

"'The doctor who had been sent for by Kenny stood over Doc pouring him a tumbler of whiskey, jotting down medical quotes in his notebook. During the final moments, when the end was approaching, Doc turned his head toward Kate and smiled. He turned up the tumbler with great fashion as he always had done in the past.

"'As the light began to fade from his eyes, he took his last breath, and heard him say, "This is funny." Then his eyes stood still, and his body relaxed. Doc was lying on his bed, dead. I remember Kate saying in a distraught voice, "The end of Holliday." The room seemed as lifeless as he was.

"'He had opened his eyes once or twice that morning, but his gaze was clouded. When I saw him open his eyes at Kate, she leaned over him straining to hear something or read something from his eyes.

Kate was trying to tell him something, though I doubt he heard her. The Colt, which he employed laid idle in the bureau, retired for all times. "Doc is at peace, Charlie. The worms won't get Doc today."

"'It is unthinkable, but during his time of dying, I realized the loss that Kate was feeling. In the beginning when I first met him in Tombstone, he had been a sporting man, usually staying among Wyatt's crowd, yet everyone who knew him was certain of his loyalty to friends.

"'Doc didn't have many friends, and he showed honor to the ones he did have. Those in the room were showing their respect for Doc. During the moment when he at last found peace, and the pain had left him, I knew he had found what he longed for. Doc had died a slow, lingering death.

"'It would surprise him to have escaped death so many times, to have died in a room in Glenwood Springs. At the end when Doc was gone, the doctor noted the time of death. "Nine fifty-five, November 8, 1887."

"'Preparations were made for a quick funeral, which would take place in a place called Linwood, a short distance by hack at two o'clock the same day. It would be a quiet procession, with the Reverend Rudolph officiating. His coffin would be elaborate with silver trimmings, donated by Glenwood's social class and friends he had made.

"'By 11 o'clock, the undertakers came to remove Doc's body from the hotel. It was the first time I had seen the physical scars the consumption had left on his body. The body was taken away. A black hearse rolled to a stop near the front entrance, and everybody came outside. Those who were standing on the boardwalk and those in the street tipped their hats to Kate as the hearse drove away.

"'Kate left Glenwood Springs after Doc's possessions were in order to be sent back to relatives in Georgia. It was a sad parting. I left November 10th, the day after Kate. Will stop by Leadville to see Bob I think.'"

It is interesting to note from the above article that several items which have been questioned over the years as to their authenticity can now quite possibly be certified as being accurate as a result of this article.

First of all, this article confirms that Kate Harony did in fact come to Doc's aid during his last days, staying with him and caring for him until the end. The article also gives a specific date (May 24, 1887) for Doc's arrival in Glenwood Springs. Prior to this article, it was known only that he had arrived in the spring of 1887.

Also confirmed by the article is the fact that Art Kendrick (Kenny) – who long claimed he was the bellhop in the Hotel Glenwood during Doc's last days and ran many errands for him – was also actually telling the truth about those experiences.

Finally, one of the most enduring legends of the Old West is also put to bed with this article which confirms that Doc did indeed utter the words "This is funny" just prior to his death, acknowledging the humor in the fact that he was dying with his boots off.

Mary K. "Big Nose Kate" Harony Cummings (second from left) was photographed in 1930 at age 80 approximately 10 years prior to her death. She lived to a ripe old age – 53 years beyond Doc's death – despite being exposed continuously to the famous gunman's contagious tuberculosis. (Sharlot Hall Museum Library / Archives, Prescott, AZ.)

Where Lie The Bones
Of John Henry Holliday?

He is one of the most celebrated figures of the old West, but today, Doc's final resting place is completely unknown. . . . or is it?

Most of the locations of the last remains of the popular figures from the old West are known quite well today. Interestingly, however, the specific location of the last remains one of the most famous old West gunmen of all time is a mystery today.

Inaccurate information also seemed to plague Doc in death just as it had in real life. His obituary was printed in a variety of newspapers, but

This tombstone, though recently replaced, originally stood in the cemetery outside Glenwood Springs, Colorado for perhaps half a century supposedly identifying the grave of Doc Holliday. Ironically, not only did the headstone not identify the specific burial plot of the famed gunman, the engraving in the headstone contained numerous errors of fact about Holliday, including his birth site, birthday, and the medical school he attended.

Grand Avenue in Glenwood Springs was photographed on June 18, 1898, a little over 10 years after Holliday's death. The gambler from Georgia strode down this street more than a few times. Visible on the right side of the street in the distance is the Hotel Glenwood in which he died.

very few if any of them printed factual information about his death. The local newspaper in Glenwood Springs, Colorado (where he died), stated that Doc was buried in Linwood Cemetery, Glenwood Springs, Colorado, at 4:00 p.m., November 8, 1887. However, the steep trail that led to the cemetery (which exists on a hilltop mesa) was impassable due to snow and ice at that time. According to records, Doc was actually buried in a temporary grave at the foot of the hill, and no one knows exactly where he is buried today.

The same Glenwood Springs newspaper also stated that many friends attended Holliday's funeral, but since he was buried the same day he died, this too is doubtful.[2] Further, both a monument and Holliday's headstone in Linwood Cemetery contained numerous mistakes when erected. It was almost as if his detractors were attempting to harass him even in death.

Tombstone, Arizona historian Ben Traywick seemed to state it best: "It is difficult to see how so many mistakes could be made on a headstone without trying."[3]

Despite the fact that a monument in Linwood Cemetery continues to proclaim that Holliday is buried "somewhere in this cemetery," most historians are convinced he was not.

One account maintains that following the spring thaw in 1888, a relative of Holliday's traveled to Glenwood Springs, retrieved the gunfighter's body, and returned with it to Georgia where it was re-interred in Oak

Hill Cemetery in Griffin, his boyhood home.

Bill Dunn, a distant relative of Holliday's, has been engaged in extensive research on the Holliday family for a number of years.

"There is no doubt in my mind why the people in Glenwood Springs don't know exactly where Doc is buried," Dunn said in an interview in 1999. "[It's because] he isn't there. Doc is buried right here in his hometown of Griffin. He was originally buried in Linwood Cemetery, but he is not there now. You just don't lose the grave of a man who held his celebrity status."

Buried In Georgia?

Some researchers believe that Doc's father, Major Henry B. Holliday (or his emissary), traveled to Glenwood Springs and claimed his son's remains. In retrospect, this is a definite possibility, since transportation of the coffin and remains could easily have been accomplished via the Denver & Rio Grand Western (D&RGW) Railroad in Glenwood Springs which was completed in 1887 – the year Holliday died. And back in Griffin, Georgia, the train depot was within a mile of Oak Hill Cemetery.

The Leadville Bar in the Hotel Denver in Glenwood Springs no doubt experienced its share of identity confusion in its day. It was photographed circa 1890s, and quite possibly was visited by Holliday prior to his demise in Glenwood Springs. (Courtesy of Frontier Historical Society)

Dunn says he believes that if it was not Major Holliday who retrieved his son's remains, he quite possibly sent his nephew, Robert Alexander Holliday, to perform the task. Doc's consort out West – Mary Katherine Harony – recalled in a later interview that one of Doc's cousins visited him in Tombstone after the shootout at the O.K. Corral. Dunn says he believes this man was Robert.

Strangely coincidental – or maybe not – is the fact that the final resting place of Major Holliday himself is also unknown today. Considering the fact that Henry Burroughs Holliday was a wealthy landowner, a decorated veteran of three wars, and the mayor of Valdosta, Georgia, it is highly unlikely that his final resting place would not have been clearly marked and definitely known today.

Major Holliday outlived his son by several years. He died on February 22, 1893 in Valdosta. Despite many years of searches, the location of his grave has eluded researchers just as has that of his famous son.

Bill Dunn maintains that he has located a marked grave for every Holliday family member in Valdosta and Griffin – all except for Major Holliday and his son, Doc. Dunn says he now believes without a doubt he has found the unmarked graves of both in Griffin's Oak Hill Cemetery.

The Plot Thickens

The two graves which Dunn says belong to Henry Burroughs and John Henry Holliday are located in the Thomas family plot. The families enjoyed a very close relationship, and Dunn says he believes the Thomas family may have agreed to an anonymous burial of Doc in their family plot to avoid vandalism of his grave.

"I believe they buried Doc in Oak Hill when he was brought back from Glenwood Springs, and Major Holliday was buried there when he died," Dunn remarks. "Why would a plot containing expensive marble markers of the Thomas family contain two concrete slab graves with no marking or identification? Could it be that they wanted them to remain anonymous?"

Osgood Miller, an employee of Clark Monument Company for forty-six years, added credence to Dunn's claim in a recent interview. He said he remembered the late Charlie McElroy – who was cemetery superintendent during the 1930s – telling him that Doc Holliday was buried in Oak Hill. Osgood said Charlie even pointed in the direction of the Thomas plot when he made the statement. Several years later, the late Griffin historian Laura Clark pointed out the same area as Doc's final resting place.

Holliday cousin Bill Dunn kneels at the gravesites of what some researchers now believe to be the final resting place of Doc Holliday and his father, Major Henry B. Holliday in Oak Hill Cemetery in Griffin. The confirmed graves of both men have eluded historians for almost a century. (Photo by Russell Underwood, courtesy of Bill Dunn)

The Hotel Glenwood at the corner of 8th and Grand was photographed circa 1887, the year of Holliday's death on the fifth floor of this structure. (Photo courtesy of Frontier Historical Society)

Retracing Doc's Footsteps
In the Colorado Rockies

Today, many of Holliday's former haunts in the West in the 1880s still exist, much as they did when he yet breathed the fresh Arizona and Colorado air.

Looking for a great vacation opportunity with lots of old West history? I recently set out on an exodus of sorts. I wanted to see the last towns in the old West in which Holliday had lived during the years prior to his death in 1887. In the end, I saw that and much more during this trip which proved to be a fascinating adventure into yesteryear.

Today, almost all serious researchers and historians know that Doc was born in Griffin, Georgia, and spent many of his formative years there and at the family's Civil War-era home in Valdosta, Georgia, to which they relocated in 1864 to escape the ravages of the war. I wanted to

Though Main Street (Harrison Ave.) is paved today, Doc Holliday enjoyed much this same view as he entered Leadville in the 1880s, pursuing the many gambling opportunities in this town. For a number of years, he lived in a room above Hyman's Saloon at 316 Harrison. This structure still stands today approximately two-thirds of the way down this street on the left. (Photo by Olin Jackson)

Another photo of Leadville from Carbonate Hill above town was taken circa 1884 near the time Doc Holliday lived in the town. (Photo courtesy of Denver Public Library Western Collection)

retrace the route Holliday had taken in the final years of his life after he had moved to the West and prior to his expiration from the ills of tuberculosis in Glenwood Springs, Colorado in 1887. I would be traveling in the reverse direction Holliday had taken, but I would be able to see many of his old haunts nonetheless.

An Arduous Journey

Driving the hundreds of desolate miles across Kansas, I couldn't help but imagine what it had been like for Holliday – sick as he was – to travel by stagecoach and on horseback to various towns in this state in the 1870s and 1880s. He traveled by train when possible, but since railroads in the West were somewhat limited at that time, he took stagecoaches to most of his destinations. He also traveled by horseback in some of the more remote areas.

I'm not certain how Doc originally traveled to Denver. He visited it a number of times early in his career out West simply because it was a more modern and civilized city than most any other in the West at that time. He supported himself by gambling, and Denver, as a result of its gold rush heritage, offered many saloons and gambling houses at which the former dentist could ply the gambling trade.

Desite the beauty of the soaring Rockies in the distance, Leadville, Colorado can have a desolate appearance on many days. This, however, did not deter the thousands of fortune-seekers who flocked to this locale in the 1870s after gold was discovered on the slopes above town. This view is toward town from the gold mines above the community. (Photo by Olin Jackson).

By the time he returned to Denver in 1882, however, he was a "Wanted" man in Arizona for his involvement in "the Vendetta Ride." He had joined Wyatt and Warren Earp, Turkey Creek Jack Johnson, Texas Jack Vermillion, Sherman McMasters and several others in hunting down the outlaws known to have been involved in the murder of Morgan Earp in Tombstone, Arizona that year.

As a result, Denver no longer was able to offer John Henry the comfortable refuge he had enjoyed in the past. After being arrested there and very nearly extradited back to Arizona, he was forced to seek out new horizons, and therefore moved on to other gold mining towns which also offered gambling opportunities.

Today, few if any of Doc's former haunts in Denver remain for the curious. Modern development has eliminated virtually all of the old hotels and saloons from yesteryear in this town. I decided not to waste my time searching for remnants of his days here.

Better Luck In Leadville

One needs only to travel the highlands of Colorado today in a comfortable automobile to understand just how uncomfortable it must have been riding in a freezing cold jarring stagecoach for hundreds of miles through the snow-covered Rocky Mountains in the 1880s. Warm comfortable restrooms at various locations and hot meals at safe comfortable restaurants were non-existent. Holliday, however, just as most other travelers at that time, was a resilient individual.

According to records, the tubercular dentist took a stage to Leadville in

1882, living there for four years (the most time he spent in any spot in the West). I wanted to visit this historic high-altitude town to see what vestiges of Holliday remain there today.

Located at 10,152 feet above sea level, this old West mining town is surrounded by Colorado's tallest peaks, and includes many historic aspects above and beyond the distinction of being one of Holliday's former residences.

The historic Tabor Opera House which still stands in town hosted many famous entertainers and celebrities over the years, including boxer Jack Dempsey, author Oscar Wilde, magician Harry Houdini and musician John Philip Sousa and his Marine Band.

The Tabor home at 116 E. 5th Street in town was built by H.A.W. (Horace) Tabor sometime around 1877. Horace and his first wife, Augusta, lived in this residence until 1881. At that time, Horace moved to the near-

TABOR OPERA HOUSE – Located next door to the old Hyman Saloon building where Holliday lived and worked, the Tabor, which opened in 1879, was said to be the grandest theater between St. Louis and San Francisco in its day. Wealthy businessman H.A.W. Tabor built the structure which seated 880 people within its luxurious interior. It hosted many notables during Leadville's heydays, including appearances by heavyweight boxing champion Jack Dempsey, author Oscar Wilde, famed magician Harry Houdini, and John Philip Sousa's Marine Band. Holliday, who thoroughly enjoyed theatrical productions, no doubt spent a fair amount of time enjoying this facility from 1882 to 1886. (Photo by Olin Jackson)

by Windsor Hotel to be near his mistress "Baby Doe." The Tabor love triangle grew into a national scandal and finally ended in a divorce between Horace and Augusta, and a marriage between Horace and Baby Doe.

Unfortunately, Tabor, who was extremely wealthy, was heavily invested in silver. In 1893, after the repeal of the Sherman Silver Act which removed silver as the metal which "backed" currency issued in the United States, a silver panic ensued, sending silver prices plummeting. Tabor, who had owned the huge Tabor Grand Building and the opulent Tabor Opera House among other properties, began a long but steady slide toward insolvency.

In 1895, Horace Tabor, amazingly, declared bankruptcy, and Baby Doe eventually began walking the streets of Leadville in rags. Also in 1895, Augusta Tabor died as a result of respiratory problems. She, however, was a millionaire at her death. Horace was a pauper.

Opened originally as the Board of Trade saloon in 1879, the facility known today as the Silver Dollar Saloon at 313 Harrison Avenue is now a novelty and collectibles shop. From 1882 to 1886 however, when it was a real saloon and gambling establishment, it was regularly patronized by Doc during his off hours when he wasn't working across the street in Hyman's Saloon. The owner of the Board of Trade was one of several individuals who bailed Doc out of jail following the Billy Allen shooting in Leadville. (Photo by Olin Jackson)

In 1884, in the building next door to the Tabor Opera House, John Henry Holliday was involved in his last gunfight. I had read about Leadville and Holliday's gunfight there, and attempted to visit the town on a previous trip to Colorado in December of 2001. An unexpected heavy snowfall, and the subsequent closure of the roads into the town, however, ultimately prevented me from visiting it at that time.

In the 1880s, Leadville was a gold and silver mining town of considerable repute. Holliday had turned to gambling which had served him well in places like Dodge City, Kansas; Tombstone Arizona; and Denver, Colorado. Leadville offered a continuation of the same gambling opportunities.

Historic But "Spartan"

As a result of the extreme elevation of this town, even I, with my healthy lungs, sometimes felt the effects of the oxygen-depleted air. I could only imagine that Holliday, with his ruined lungs, must have struggled considerably. He is known to have contracted pneumonia several times while living here, but amazingly survived the illness each time.

In 1884, the population of Leadville was approximately 20,000 (not counting "soiled doves" as the towns literature proclaims). According to records, it had 92 saloons, 61 lawyers, numerous gambling houses and brothels, and 8 churches. A number of these same buildings still exist today.

My accommodations for the next few days in Leadville would be at the historic Delaware Hotel in the heart of the town. The Delaware has reigned as an architectural cornerstone of Leadville's National Historic District for years, and is often referred to as the "Crown Jewel" of the town. According to this interesting inn's literature, it has played host to a number of notables over the years, including Butch Cassidy who reportedly roomed there during one notorious visit to the town.

As with Tombstone, Arizona, Leadville, Colorado – due to its somewhat isolated and inhospitable location – has changed little from the old West days of Holliday. There has been very little "modern development" over the years. Some of the old buildings have disappeared as a result of fire and general neglect, and occasionally, a new church or a new saloon – designed much the same as the old ones – has been built, but little else has changed. The area is simply too unattractive, climate-wise.

To understand this, all one has to do is walk to a second or third floor room in a hotel in the town. Following this effort, a full four or five-minute recuperation will be required by almost anyone over 35. For this reason, I hereby offer the following advice to future travelers to this site: The Delaware Hotel has three stories of rooms – but there is no elevator in the facility. Therefore, reserve your room in advance – and get a room on the first floor. Otherwise, you will have no one to blame but yourself for your sufferings as you trudge up the stairs of this facility.

My room was on the third floor, and one must experience a labored walk up two flights of narrow stairs in oxygen-depleted circumstances before one can truly appreciate the luxury of first floor accommodations at 10,000+ feet above sea level. Each trip back to my room required the aforementioned four or five-minute rest at the top of the stairs before I could even advance to my room.

Though some mining continues in Leadville today, the town now derives most of its income from tourism, and judging from the somewhat depressed appearance of the community during my stay, it seems to be struggling financially. Long gone are the fast times and fast money generated by the mineral wealth of the area in the 1880s.

The Delaware was built in 1886, and it may or may not have been patronized by John Henry Holliday. He left Leadville in 1887, spending the final months of his life in Glenwood Springs prior to his death there in November of that year. If he did not visit the Delaware, however, it would be one of the few buildings in town which escaped his attentions, for he was surprisingly active in the community during the approximate four years he lived there, moving from saloon to saloon to ply his trade.

Doc's Old Hotel

During my first day in Leadville, I walked down Main Street (Harrison Ave.) to 316 Harrison to the old hotel/saloon (originally Mannie Hyman's Saloon) in which Doc had lived and worked from 1882 to 1887. This saloon was also the site of Holliday's last gunfight in which he shot (and almost killed) Billy Allen in 1884.

As of this writing, this structure is owned by Mary McVicar who has conducted considerable research on Holliday. She proved to be a captivating conversationalist on the subject too. Many of the books and other materials published about Holliday today quote her research.

Though some historians question their authenticity, a number of dental tools and at least one pistol supposedly once owned by Holliday are now owned by Ms. McVicar and displayed on the walls of the former saloon.

Doc's room in this historic building was upstairs on the northwest corner. It is seven-by-fourteen feet in size and is open to the public on occasion for viewing.

In the 1880s, Mannie Hyman rented nine rooms in this building to various individuals. Holliday's room included a view through the front window of the snow-covered peaks of the Rocky Mountains.

Although Doc was a faro dealer in Hyman's, he also regularly gambled himself in John G. Morgan's Board of Trade Saloon across the street, as well as in a number of other saloons and gambling houses in town. The Board of Trade building, which also still stands, is called the Silver Dollar Saloon as of this writing.

The Last Gunfight

In his day, Holliday developed a strong friendship with the Board of Trade's owners – John Morgan and Col. Samuel Houston – and it later proved to be a valuable association. When he was arrested for shooting

Billy Allen, Holliday was destitute, and so sick he could no longer support himself as a gambler. As a result, he could not raise bail, and undoubtedly would have been forced to endure a long wait in jail prior to his trial had not Morgan and Houston stepped forward.

Together, the two merchants quickly posted the $5,000 bail money – a considerable sum in the 1880s – and Holliday was released to return to his sick-bed until the day of his trial. He subsequently was acquitted of the charges against him.

As I strolled about the main room of the old Hyman saloon, imagining the circumstances of the gunfight, Ms. McVicar pointed out many details concerning the incident, showing me the spot at which Holliday had stood as he fired, and the spot at which Allen had fallen after being wounded.

Billy Allen was an old enemy of Holliday's, dating back to the Tombstone days in 1881. He (Allen) was a friend of the Clantons, a family of outlaws who had opposed the Earps and Holliday in the gunfight near the O.K. Corral.

Allen had also testified against Holliday at the Inquest following the shooting at the O.K. Corral, and a number of individuals – including Doc himself – believed Allen had fired several shots at him during the Tombstone fracas. For this and other reasons, Allen and Holliday were anything but friends.

By the time Doc and Allen met again in Leadville, Holliday was much weaker and sicker, and Allen no doubt saw an opportunity to gain a reputation for himself as the individual who finally got the drop on the famed gunman. It was a confrontation which was almost inevitable.

Despite the fact that Holliday was almost defenseless by this time (He had ceased carrying a gun, since he could not afford the fine if he were caught carrying a concealed weapon.), he seemed to find an inner resolve which enabled him to deal with the situation. After being publicly bullied and humiliated by Allen and his cronies on a number of occasions, Doc finally received word that his tormentor was coming to pay him a final visit. In the end, however, Allen ended up writhing on the floor, and Doc was uninjured. It was interesting to visit the building where that drama had finally played out.

Leadville was very cold (in the 30s the day I visited in September of 2003). There was snow on the ground and more snow falling. I can only assume it was much the same during Holliday's stay, and despite the liveliness of the saloons and gambling opportunities at the time, the town must have been a very forbidding place to live in the 1880s.

Doc spent a few days with Wyatt and Warren Earp and Dan Tipton in Gunnison, Colorado, as the men eluded "law enforcement authorities" from Arizona in the summer of 1882 after what came to be known as "the vendetta ride." Virginia Avenue in Gunnison was photographed here circa 1890s, and undoubtedly was little-changed from the time when Doc and Wyatt strode these streets. (Denver Public Library, Western History Department)

Gunning For Gunnison

Our next destination was Gunnison. We arose at 7:15 a.m. the next morning and enjoyed our last breakfast in the famed Delaware. After loading up our Dodge Durango, we headed south on U.S. 24 to U.S. 285 and thence to U.S. 50. This was an amazingly beautiful drive, and should not be missed if ever one has the opportunity to enjoy it. Huge towering snow-capped peaks and very striking rock formations all along this route make it a fascinatingly scenic route.

We finally reached Monarch Pass high in the mountains, and I thought at first that we were going to have to use snow-chains to make it through the pass. Fortunately there had not been an accumulation of ice, and so the chains were not necessary. During winter months, however, snow chains very definitely would be required in the higher elevations such as this.

We drove through deep snow for a number of miles (this was in September when the temperatures were in the 80s and 90s in Georgia) and finally dropped below the snow line again on the other side of the pass.

We finally reached Gunnison after a full day's ride. I could see why this spot was chosen by Wyatt and Warren Earp and Doc as a spot to spend the summer of 1882. They had just finished their "Vendetta Ride" in Arizona, and were on the run from what at the time were corrupt Arizona authorities.

The remote and isolated location of Gunnison offered just the peace and solitude the Earps and Doc no doubt were seeking at that time. This tiny mountain community is located in a broad, somewhat fertile valley at the top of the Colorado Rockies. It would have been very difficult to reach – especially by someone on horseback in the 1880s.

According to records, the Earps camped outside town for the entire summer, but Doc, preferring an easier life in the hotels of Denver, only remained for a week or so. Gunnison becomes brutally cold in the winter (with temperatures reportedly at minus 20 degrees Fahrenheit), so camping in any season other than summer simply is not feasible.

Doc moved on to Denver for a few months before eventually traveling to Leadville. Wyatt eventually drifted back southwestward to California.

Hooray For Ouray

I continued the drive along beautiful Blue Mesa Lake (Colorado's largest) for many miles, witnessing still more amazing scenery. This drive

Ouray was yet another mining town in which gold and silver were sought in the late 1800s, and Doc Holliday and Wyatt and Warren Earp all quite likely passed through it in their wanderings in the early 1880s. (Photo by Olin Jackson)

from Leadville to Ouray and on to Telluride has to be one of the most beautiful in America.

I turned onto U.S. Highway 550 and after additional miles, finally reached the next destination – historic Ouray, Colorado. This town also was a gold-mining community after the precious yellow metal was discovered there in 1875.

It is not known by this writer if Holliday traveled to this vicinity during his wanderings to various gambling opportunities in Colorado. However, he crisscrossed this vicinity in the 1880s, and therefore could easily have passed time in Ouray, but if he did, it was an obscure visit at best, since no mention of it has been found thusfar in historic records. That absence of a record of his visit to this town, however, means nothing, since much of Doc's wanderings were done with no mention or record of his visits whatsoever.

Conversely, the Earps more than likely did pass through Ouray on their way back southwestward through Colorado to California in 1882. The town, at the very least, was along the route they would have taken from Gunnison. I followed (and could often see to one side of the highway) historic markers identifying the old stagecoach route to this town for much of the ride.

The magnificent surroundings of Ouray – the San Juan Mountains – are breath-taking to say the least, rising to 14,000 feet. A photograph or verbal description simply does not do this area justice. These peaks form an unbelievable back-drop for the elegant Victorian homes and old West commercial buildings of this town, many of which were built between 1880 and 1900.

The population of the town is only 800 permanent residents year-round, and that's one of the things I liked best about this locale. It not only is an unbelievably scenic area, but a very peaceful one as well. It is located at 7,770 feet so it's high enough that you know you're in the Colorado Rockies, but low enough to have pleasing weather year-round.

A typical summer day in Ouray is sunny, with temperatures in the 70s and 80s. Evening temperatures range in the 50s. A typical winter averages 140 inches of snowfall and the days are sunny and bright with highs averaging in the 40s and lows in the high teens. It gets plenty cold enough to provide a favorable environment for lots of snow, but it's not unbearably cold – just the way I like it. Although it is not necessary, it is strongly advisable to drive only a four-wheel drive vehicle with snow tires or chains during the winter.

The stark beauty of the soaring Rockies coupled with the historic landscape of downtown Ouray, Colorado, won it the honor of usage as a backdrop for some scenes in the major motion picture "True Grit," starring John Wayne, Glen Campbell, Kim Darby, and Robert Duvall. Some of the courthouse scenes in the movie were filmed in the historic Ouray courthouse in the center of town. (Photo by Olin Jackson)

My accommodations in Ouray were at the St. Elmo Hotel. This marvelous old inn near the downtown area was built in 1898, and – just as many other historic buildings in this town – still exists almost as it did when built over 100 years ago. I was not able to learn if one of the aged commercial buildings on the old main street of this town once served as a hotel in which a wandering John Henry Holliday might have passed time. I did, however discover that another historic figure from the old West spent time here.

True Grit

The next morning, we emerged for a visit to the old downtown area of Ouray. It was because of the scenic beauty and old West atmosphere here that selected spots in Ouray and the adjacent community of Ridgway were used in the filming of the 1969 major motion picture, *True Grit.* Starring John Wayne, Kim Darby, Glen Campbell and Robert Duvall, this award-winning movie is still one of the most popular Westerns ever filmed, and the "Duke" earned an Academy Award for his performance.

Interestingly, the old courthouse in the middle of Ouray was the site at which the *True Grit* courthouse scenes with Wayne were filmed. As we were leaving this town several days later, I was able to stop at Ridgway a few miles away to see where Wayne had performed in other scenes from *True Grit* filmed in that town.

I later traveled to other scenic destinations in Colorado, New Mexico and Texas on this same trip. The only other town I visited, however – which was also visited by Holliday – was Dallas, Texas, ironically where Doc's travels in the old West had begun so many years ago. Today, just as in Denver, Holliday's tracks in fast-moving Dallas have also been obscured forever by modern development.

During my visit, I made additional stops at historic Telluride. While I was there, I was able to visit the old San Miguel Valley Bank building (which still stands on Main Street in Telluride) which was robbed by Butch Cassidy and three accomplices in 1889, two years after Doc's death.

Following my departure from Telluride, I drove down State Highway

The historic town of Telluride – a popular ski resort today – was also an early mining town frequented by gamblers and roughnecks from throughout the West in the 1880s. The old San Miguel Valley Bank building (second from left) still stands on Main Street. This depository became the first victim of the Wild Bunch - Butch Cassidy and three accomplices - who held it up in 1889, two years after Doc's death. (Photo by Olin Jackson)

This photo has been published and identified as John Henry Holliday for many years, and is still identified as such today in television history programs and in many books. In fact, it is actually John Escapule of Bisbee, Arizona who lived at roughly the same time as Doc. (Courtesy of John Tindall)

145 which is an ancient travel route through the Rockies, originally cut by migratory animals in prehistory. This trail subsequently fell into use by Native Americans and still later by white settlers as a stage coach route. According to records, Cassidy traversed this route many times as he rustled horses to sell in Telluride. He also followed it as he fled Telluride after robbing the bank there in 1889.

It is not known by this writer if Doc Holliday traversed this vicinity in southwestern Colorado, but Wyatt and Warren Earp almost certainly did. If you're looking for an interesting vacation in some very historic old West towns, visit the places described above. You'll be glad you did, and along the way, you'll gain an appreciation for the rugged life endured by those hardy travelers of yesteryear – particularly John Henry Holliday.

A tourism sign in downtown Telluride. (Photo by Olin Jackson)

THE TELLURIDE MOUNTAINS CONTAIN 350 MILES OF TUNNELS, ENOUGH TO REACH FROM SAN FRANCISCO TO LOS ANGELES. BILLIONS OF DOLLARS IN GOLD, SILVER, COPPER, LEAD AND ZINC HAVE BEEN PRODUCED HERE SINCE 1880 AND THE AREA IS STILL BEING MINED

Doc's Acquaintances

What do we know today that can be confirmed as factual information regarding the life and acquaintances of John Henry Holliday? Well, according to Doc's first cousin, it's a short list.

For more than a century, Georgia native and old West gunman Doc Holliday has acquired a reputation as difficult to dissect as the gunfight at the O.K. Corral which holds the dubious distinction of having been termed "the most confusing 15 seconds in American history." Even more conflicting, however, are the various modern descriptions of the relationships Doc had with his acquaintances in the West.

Fanned by dime novels, rumor, innumerable erroneous articles, books and movies, the brushfire that supposedly represents the real Doc Holliday continues to burn unabated.

Susan McKey Thomas is Holliday's first cousin once-removed. Perhaps it is appropriate that her educated, scrupulously studied opinions of Doc become, if not the last word, at least a part of the final sentence.

"Big Nose Kate"

Aside from the famous incident at the O.K. Corral in Tombstone, Arizona, in October of 1881, one of the few things about which most historians agree regarding Holliday was his intimate relationship with Mary Katherine Harony (Haroney) Cummings, a.k.a. Kate Elder, a prostitute who was known by at least seven different identities during her life. She appears to have been the gunfighter's only romantic interest of consequence after he left Georgia.

Though she passes no judgment on the Holliday-Elder coupling, Ms. Thomas says with no reservation that no official marriage ever took place regarding the pair, in spite of the fact that many sources accept the marriage as fact and Harony herself was vehement in her assertions that she was Doc's widow.

Ms. Thomas maintains a long list of evidence to back up her assertion to the contrary.

"There are so many reasons not to believe he was ever married to Katie Elder," Ms. Thomas explained in an interview in 2001. "When she told the story, she said they were married in Valdosta, supposedly on a visit in 1880, and she gave a date. Well, the marriages of that period are available on record, and there is no record of any marriage between Doc and Katie."

Thomas's argument is augmented by the fact that Doc Holliday almost certainly never returned to Georgia after traveling to the West. Thomas maintained that most of what Doc's immediate family even knew of the prodigal son after he went West was gleaned from *The Valdosta Daily Times* newspaper.

Then there is the family *Bible*.

"I have an authentic copy of the records in the family Bible," Ms. Thomas continued. "Now his father was a meticulous man, and in that Bible are entries of births, deaths – anything that pertained to the family. The major almost certainly would have entered the marriage – whether he approved of it or not – and he did not enter anything about such a marriage."

Although Doc Holliday did not correspond with his Valdosta relatives, it is a matter of record that he did write regularly to his first cousin, Sister Mary Melanie, a member of the Sisters of Mercy convent who lived in Augusta and Atlanta. There is a great probability that Sister Mary would have passed along the news of such a marriage, unless Doc specifically instructed her to the contrary, which of course is always possible.

According to Ms. Thomas, there is even more evidence of the absence of such a marriage. "Katie told an interviewer about their relationship, and not only did she not know the names of Doc's family, but she got Doc's birth date wrong – by about 10 years."

Further evidence rests in the fact that census records from 1880 show Doc Holliday residing in Prescott, Arizona, with two other men, one of whom was John Gosper, acting governor of Arizona Territory.

Regardless of the circumstances, Doc did enjoy a long and sometimes combative relationship with Mary Katherine Harony, traveling on many adventures with her.

The Earp Family

As far as Doc Holliday's relationship with the Earp family is concerned, it seems a little hazy too, which is not surprising under the circumstances. After an alliance with the Earps which lasted at least four years, Holliday parted ways with Wyatt in Albuquerque, New Mexico in 1882. By that time, Morgan Earp – a very close friend of Doc's – had been assassinated in Tombstone, and brother Virgil Earp had also been shot in the back and relegated to a life as a cripple in Los Angeles, California.

"I can't really say if they parted as friends or as friendly enemies," Thomas added. "I'm not certain, but from everything I can gather, my impression is that they just reached a parting of the ways. Sometimes friendships just reach a point where everything that can be said has been said, and people just go their separate ways. I really think that's probably what happened. Maybe there was no reason to continue their partnership after what happened [in the gunfight and its aftermath in Tombstone]."

Thomas suggested the bond between Holliday and the Earps may well have been little more than a friendship of necessity in what then was virtually a lawless environment, making a parting of the ways less than surprising. In point of fact, however, documents today indicate that Wyatt and Doc had a falling out over an unflattering comment Doc may have made concerning Wyatt's respect for Jewish traditions. (By that time, Wyatt's bond with his future common-law wife, Josephine Sara Marcus, a Jewess, was quite strong.)

Ms. Thomas also said some insight may be gained into Holliday's life and personality – as well as to his relationship with the Earps – from a letter Thomas said she received from a very elderly George Earp, dated December 21, 1958. George was a descendant from Nicholas Earp's (patriarch of the Earp brothers) first marriage.

Responding to a letter from the McKey family written after an appearance on The $64,000 Question quiz show that year, George Earp wrote Thomas that he had known Holliday for a very brief period in Dodge City.

"When I knew him, he was always a gentlemanly fellow," Earp wrote. "He was always wanting to die and apparently wanted to be killed. That is why he always wanted to join Wyatt Earp in those gun battles."

Unfortunately, much – if not all – of the information obtained from George Earp appears to have been falsified in an attempt by the distant Earp to enjoy a portion of the notoriety experienced by his forebears. Today, it is believed that George Earp never even knew Doc Holliday personally.

Bat Masterson

Ms. Thomas has a much more definite opinion about Bat Masterson, who, like the Earps, was allied with Holliday during the heady days of Dodge City, Kansas, where Masterson served as a city marshal.

"For some reason, Bat Masterson didn't like Doc," Thomas asserted. "He seemed to like the Earps, but he definitely didn't like Doc."

Ms. Thomas said she also blames much of the Holliday bad press on Masterson, who went on to write about the period known as the "Wild West" in respected publications such as *The New York Times*. After living in the West for many years, Masterson later moved back East to New York where he went to work as a writer for the Times. He ultimately died at his desk, a worn-out old man.

"Bat Masterson never wrote anything complimentary about Doc," Thomas added. "He made some very disparaging remarks about Doc." Though Ms. Thomas did her best to maintain a position as an impartial historian, she said she clearly saw Masterson as a self-serving opportunist eager to secure a place for himself as one of the heroes of the period when in fact, some sources describe Masterson's law enforcement skills as lax or worse.

"Bat defended himself [in the newspaper] and he had a big audience. Poor old Doc just died young and had no one to defend him."

Movie Portrayals

As far as the movies about Doc Holliday are concerned, Ms. Thomas said she believed actor Val Kilmer – who researched Holliday extensively for his role in the 1993 major motion picture *Tombstone* – may have provided the most accurate portrayal of the man.

"It's obvious that Val thoroughly enjoyed the characterization," Thomas stated. "Of course, some of what he portrayed was valid and some was not so valid. But it was obvious he had done his homework."

Thomas said that in general, she regarded almost all the other movies about Holliday to be wildly inaccurate as well as simply poor cinema. She critiqued actor Dennis Quaid's take on Holliday in the 1994 movie *Wyatt Earp* as "horrible, just horrible. . . an absolute waste of time."

Another aspect of Holliday's life upon which history buffs disagree wildly is the circumstances of his death. Thomas said a letter, dated June 12, 1973, addressed to her, nailed down with probable finality that information.

The letter quotes A.E. Axtell, city manager of Glenwood Springs, Colorado, where Holliday died on November 8, 1887, after spending two months in and out of consciousness at the Hotel Glenwood. Axtell tells of former Glenwood Springs Mayor Art Kendricks, who reportedly worked as a busboy at the hotel during the time of Holliday's death.

Last Days

Axtell said Kendricks told of carrying bottles of whiskey to Holliday's room and each time being tipped a dime. According to Kendricks, when Holliday finally died, only the busboy and two others attended the funeral.

This seems to cement Ms. Thomas's argument against Mary Katherine Harony Cummings (a.k.a. Katie Elder), who claimed she was with Holliday for the last two months of his life. Still, many sources, and at least one published newspaper account (*Oklahoma Headlight*, February

William Barclay "Bat" Masterson, to put it lightly, was never a fan of John Henry "Doc" Holliday. Though Masterson helped Holliday in several perilous situations, he did it solely as a favor to his friend, Wyatt Earp. As a result, Masterson, who had dabbled in newspaper writing since the 1880s, wrote numerous unflattering articles about Holliday up until his (Masterson's) death in 1921. During the 1890s, Masterson was in Denver, Colorado, where he worked as a sports editor. By the dawning of the 20th century, he had been reduced to the stature of a drunken relic of the Old West, with very similar qualities that he had so despised in Holliday. He was booted out of Denver around 1902, never to return.

14, 1899) paint the situation in a different light, stating unequivocally that Kate was present, attending to Holliday and spending what little savings she had to pay the hotel bill, and finally, after his death, gathering Holliday's belongings and shipping them home to his relatives in Georgia.

It is known that Kate was in northwestern Colorado at roughly the same time as Doc's death, since records have been passed down of time she spent in the Crystal Valley region of Colorado near the mining town of Aspen. If she had been that near to Doc during his last days, it is difficult to imagine that she would not at least have paid him a final visit.

And what about the long-standing claim that at the end of his life, Doc regained consciousness just long enough to look at his bare feet and utter the words "This is funny" then take one last breath and die?

Ms. Thomas won't even wait for the question about that incident to be finished.

"The man was in a coma!" she exclaims. "Really, I don't think he regained consciousness for those few seconds just to say that." She shakes her head in disbelief at what she clearly considers an absurdity.

Doc's Actual Gunfights

He was involved in numerous affrays over the years, but many shootings attributed to Doc either never happened at all, or were done by other individuals.

Over the years, as legends grew throughout the Old West, the reputations of many noted gunmen invariably exceeded the actual circumstances of their experiences quite significantly. John Henry "Doc" Holliday was no exception, being credited with many more shootings and deaths than he was ever involved with.

According to Karen Holliday Tanner (*Doc Holliday: A Family Portrait*, University of Oklahoma Press, 1998) who has extensively researched the experiences of her famous forebear, Doc can be documented as having been involved only in the following incidents:

He was a participant in gunfights between himself and Charles Austin in Dallas, Texas, and with Henry Kahn in Breckenridge, with Milt Joyce in Tombstone, and with Billy Allen in Leadville. None of these shootings involved fatalities, but all resulted in wounded participants.

Doc was indicted in the Austin case and found "Not Guilty." In the shooting incident with Milt Joyce a charge of "Assault With a Deadly Weapon With Intent To Kill" was dismissed. For the misdemeanor charge of "Assault and Battery" Doc paid a $20 fine. He was also fined in the Kahn shooting and acquitted in the Billy Allen shooting.

Regarding the killing of Ed Bailey at Fort Griffin, Texas, and the shooting of Charlie White in Las Vegas, New Mexico, no charges were ever brought against Doc for those incidents.

As a result of her research, Ms. Tanner admits that it quite likely was Doc who ended the days of Old Man Clanton – the leader of the outlaw Clantons in Tombstone, Arizona Territory in the 1880s.

It is a documented fact that Doc definitely fired the shot that killed Tom McLaury, and he delivered at least one of the three fatal shots which ended the life of Frank McLaury in the October 26, 1881 shooting near the O.K. Corral.

Finally, Doc may or may not have been involved in other killings during what later came to be known as "the Vendetta Ride," when Wyatt and Warren Earp, Doc, Texas Jack Vermillion, Turkey Creek Jack Johnson and others sought out the killers of Morgan Earp, ending forever the days of the organized gang of outlaws which had frequented the Tombstone area in the 1870s and 1880s.

A Doc Holliday TimeLine (1851-1887)

- 1851: John Henry Holliday was born on August 21, in Griffin, Georgia to Henry Burroughs Holliday and Alice Jane McKey.

- 1864: Major Henry B. Holliday sells all his property and moves his family from Griffin to Valdosta, Georgia to escape the Yankee troops advancing on Atlanta.

- 1866: Alice Jane McKey Holliday, Doc's mother, dies in September. His father remarries a scant three months later.

- 1870: Doc enrolls in the Pennsylvania School of Dental Surgery at Philadelphia.

- 1872: Doc graduates from dental college.

- 1873: Doc learns he has tuberculosis. Decides to move to the West, and travels to Dallas, Texas.

- 1874: Doc arrested in Dallas for gambling. Moves to Denison, Texas.

- 1875: In a New Year's Day shooting, Doc is arrested and charged with "Assault" and "Intent To Murder" Charles Austin in Dallas. Tried and acquitted and leaves town. Indicted for gambling at Fort Griffin, Texas.

- 1876: Travels to Denver, Colorado under the identity of "Tom McKey." Knifes gambler Budd Ryan. Returns to Texas.

- 1877: Arrested three times in Dallas for gambling. Later meets Wyatt Earp for the first time at Shaughnessey's Saloon in Fort Griffin. Reportedly kills Ed Bailey in Fort Griffin, but no charges ever brought.

- 1878: Doc moves to Dodge City with Kate Elder (a.k.a. Mary Katherine Harony). Saves Wyatt Earp's life. Travels to Trinidad, Colorado and Las Vegas, New Mexico.

- 1879: Doc participates in what came to be known as the "Royal Gorge War." Opens a saloon in Las Vegas. May or may not have been involved in the shooting of Mike Gordon. Indicted for running a gambling operation and carrying a deadly weapon. Leaves Las Vegas for Prescott, Arizona with the Earps.

■ 1880: Returns to Las Vegas. Shoots Charlie White; wound only superficial. No charges ever brought to bear. Again arrested for carrying a deadly weapon. Returns to Prescott where he rooms with acting Governor John J. Gosper. Later moves to Tombstone where he is involved in an altercation with Johnny Tyler and a gunfight and brutal fist-fight with Milt Joyce. A charge of "Assault With A Deadly Weapon With Intent To Kill" was ultimately dismissed.

■ 1881: Doc helps his friend Wyatt as the two defend the arrested Johnny-Behind-The Deuce. Accused and arrested for robbery and murder involving a stage coach robbery in Benson. Case dismissed. Involved in what came to be known as the "Gunfight at the O.K. Corral." Arrested for this shooting and acquitted in the Judge Spicer hearing and Inquest.

■ 1882: Doc joins Wyatt and Warren Earp, Turkey Creek Jack Johnson, Texas Jack Vermillion, Sherman McMasters and others in what came to be known as the "Vendetta Ride" in Arizona. Present at the killings of Frank Stillwell, Florentino Cruz, and Curly Bill Brocius. Flees Arizona with the Earp Faction. Quarrels with Wyatt Earp in Albuquerque, New Mexico. Travels to Trinidad with Dan Tipton. Arrested in Denver, Colorado, for extradition back to Arizona, but rescued by Bat Masterson. Travels to Gunnison, Salida, Pueblo, and Leadville, then back to Denver.

■ 1883-1886: Lives in Leadville. Involved in his last gunfight as he shoots Billy Allen in Hyman's Saloon in Leadville. Tried for the Billy Allen shooting and acquitted. Travels back and forth to Denver several times. During final visit to Denver sees Wyatt Earp for the last time and is arrested for vagrancy. Returns to Leadville.

■ 1887: Moves to Glenwood Springs. Dies of consumption (galloping tuberculosis) on November 8, at the age of 36. Buried someplace "near Linwood Cemetery" in Glenwood Springs.

Full Name Index

Subject Index